D1008847

THE WIT

AND WISDOM

OF

RONALD

REAGAN

EDITED BY CAROL KELLY-GANGI

FALL RIVER PRESS

New York

*To my father, Howard Kelly,
with a heart full of love and gratitude*

FALL RIVER PRESS

New York

An Imprint of Sterling Publishing
387 Park Avenue South
New York, NY 10016

FALL RIVER PRESS and the distinctive Fall River Press logo are registered trademarks
of Barnes & Noble, Inc.

Compilation © 2012 by Carol Kelly-Gangi

Jacket and book design by Scott Russo

All photographs Courtesy Ronald Reagan Library

ISBN 978-1-4351-3941-1 (print format)
ISBN 978-1-4351-3944-2 (ebook)

Distributed in Canada by Sterling Publishing
c/o Canadian Manda Group, 165 Dufferin Street
Toronto, Ontario, Canada M6K 3H6
Distributed in the United Kingdom by GMC Distribution Services
Castle Place, 166 High Street, Lewes, East Sussex, England BN7 1XU
Distributed in Australia by Capricorn Link (Australia) Pty. Ltd.
P.O. Box 704, Windsor, NSW 2756, Australia

For information about custom editions, special sales, and premium and
corporate purchases, please contact Sterling Special Sales at 800-805-5489 or
specialsales@sterlingpublishing.com.

Manufactured in the United States of America

2 4 6 8 10 9 7 5 3 1

www.sterlingpublishing.com

CONTENTS

Introduction 5

Early Years 9

Democracy and Government 17

Freedom, Equality, Law and Order, and Justice 25

America 37

Politics 45

The Presidency 55

Peace, War, the Military, and Foreign Policy 69

The Economy, Business, and Labor 79

Communism and the Soviet Union 89

Family, Friends, and Life's Pleasures 97

Education, Knowledge, and Information 109

Religion 115

Poverty and Riches 121

Wit and Wisdom 127

The Legacy of Ronald Reagan 143

Chronology 161

INTRODUCTION

Ronald Reagan was at a crossroads in the mid-1950s. After five years of working in radio broadcasting, and close to twenty years working as a movie actor, he found he wasn't happy with the movie scripts he was being offered. He wasn't interested in acting in a television series, and he didn't want to relocate his family to New York to act on Broadway. Then an opportunity presented itself, a fortuitous turn in the road that sent Reagan on a path that would lead him all the way to the presidency of the United States. He was offered a job from the General Electric Company to host a weekly dramatic program called *The General Electric Theater*. As part of the job, Reagan was asked to tour GE plants around the nation, where he would meet with employees, speak to them in small groups, and retell some stories from his Hollywood days. From 1954 to 1962, he visited 139 plants and met with more than 250,000 employees, listening to their concerns and rethinking his own views about the role and size of the federal government and the impact it was having on the lives of Americans. His speeches became less and less about Hollywood and more and more about his newly formulated political views.

By 1960, he realized that the Democratic Party, of which he was a lifelong member, no longer represented the views he now believed were key to America's future success. And in 1962, he officially registered as a member of the Republican Party.

In 1964, Reagan gave the speech that would launch his political career. It was in support of Barry Goldwater's bid for the presidency. In his speech, Reagan challenged Americans to face up to the never-ending expansion of the federal government and its intrusion into their lives, and to the Democrats' tendency toward the socialization of America. The speech firmly cemented Reagan's stature as a man with a bright vision for America based on a new breed of Republican conservatism. Within two years, Reagan was elected governor of California in an overwhelming victory. After serving two terms as governor, Reagan made his first serious bid for the White House in 1976. Though he lost the Republican nomination to President Gerald Ford, his strong showing in the election created the framework for his next presidential bid.

By 1980, Reagan's time had come. He won the presidential election in a crushing victory over Jimmy Carter, and was reelected in 1984 in another landslide election. Reagan's vision of reducing the size and scope of the federal government, removing undue restrictions from business, and reestablishing the might of America's military resonated with millions of Americans. When he left the White House in 1989, it was with the highest presidential approval rating since Franklin Delano Roosevelt.

The Wit and Wisdom of Ronald Reagan gathers hundreds of quotations from Ronald Reagan from his speeches, autobiographies, letters, and other writings. In these excerpts, Reagan boldly expresses his optimism about the bright future of America and of the American dream; he speaks passionately about the freedom, equality, and justice that are central to the American landscape. He also shares his deeply held views about the role of the federal government, which he believes should be for the people and not in control of the people. In other selections, he speaks prophetically about the downfall of the Soviet system and of the vital need to secure peace through maintaining a strong defense. Still other excerpts offer a more personal glimpse into Reagan. He eloquently expresses his love and gratitude for Nancy, shares the joys and frustrations of parenting, and recalls with fondness his early family life and the gifts he received from each of his parents. Reagan also shares his views on the path to a strong economy, the value of education, the role of religion in our lives, and the nature of politics. Finally, there is a grouping of quotations in which world leaders, historians, journalists, family members, and friends offer their memories and insights into Reagan the man and his enduring legacy.

With a vision, pragmatism, wit, and optimism all his own, Reagan started a revolution that has left an indelible mark on America. *The Wit and Wisdom of Ronald Reagan* invites readers to revisit the words of our fortieth president in hopes that they will continue to inspire and once again ignite the belief in a better tomorrow for the land he loved so much.

—CAROL KELLY-GANGI
Rumson, New Jersey, 2011

EARLY YEARS

He looks like a fat little Dutchman. But who knows,
he might grow up to be president some day.

—Jack Reagan, upon the birth of his son Ronald, who was
nicknamed "Dutch" thereafter, from *An American Life:
The Autobiography* by Ronald Reagan

Even before I started school, at the age of five, I learned
to read. I can't claim special talent; it came about simply
because my mother took the time to sit down every night
and read books to us, following each word with a finger,
while we watched over her shoulder.

—*Where's the Rest of Me?* by Ronald Reagan with Richard G. Hubler

I confess, I was not as attentive as I might have been during
my classroom days. I seem to remember my parents being
told, "Young Ron is trying—very trying."

—Remarks at the annual convention of the National Parent Teacher
Association, Albuquerque, New Mexico, June 15, 1983

Although I always had lots of playmates, during those
first years in Dixon I was a little introverted and probably
a little slow in making really close friends. In some ways
I think this reluctance to get close to people never left me
completely. I've never had trouble making friends, but
I've been inclined to hold back a little of myself, reserving
it for myself. As I'd done in the attic in Galesburg,
I found a lot of enjoyment during those first years in
Dixon in solitary ways—reading, studying wildlife,
and exploring the local wilderness.

—*An American Life: The Autobiography* by Ronald Reagan

When I was a child, we moved a lot. My father was constantly
searching for a better life and I was forever the new kid
in school. During one period of four years, I attended
four different schools. We moved to wherever
my father's ambition took him.

—*An American Life: The Autobiography* by Ronald Reagan

I was eleven years old the first time I came home to find my
father flat on his back on the front porch and no one there
to lend a hand but me. He was drunk, dead to the world.
I stood over him for a minute or two. I wanted to let myself
in the house and go to bed and pretend he wasn't there.
Oh, I wasn't ignorant of his weakness. I don't know at what
age I knew what the occasional absences or the loud voices in
the night meant, but up till now my mother, Nelle, or my
brother handled the situation and I was a child in bed with
the privilege of pretending sleep. . . . I felt myself fill with
grief for my father at the same time I was feeling sorry for
myself. Seeing his arms spread out as if he were crucified—as
indeed he was—his hair soaking with melting snow, snoring
as he breathed, I could feel no resentment against him. . . .
Opening the door, I managed to drag him inside and get
him to bed. In a few days he was the bluff, hearty man
I knew and loved and will always remember.

—*WHERE'S THE REST OF ME?* by Ronald Reagan with Richard G. Hubler

He [Jack Reagan] was a restless man, burning with ambition
to succeed. When I left home at seventeen to go to college,
we had never lived in a house we owned; it was twenty years
afterward that I was able to bring him out to Hollywood and
present him with the clear deed to a small house and lot,
the first piece of real estate he had ever owned. It was the
most satisfying gift of my life.

—*WHERE'S THE REST OF ME?* by Ronald Reagan with Richard G. Hubler

As teenagers, Neil and I began calling our parents by their first names. It started one day when Neil, after enlisting my backing, told the folks that since we were such a close family, wasn't it appropriate for the two of us to address them as Jack and Nelle? They were probably a little shocked at first, but they consented to it, and after a while I think they liked the special familiarity it gave the four of us.

—*An American Life: The Autobiography* by Ronald Reagan

Moon [Neil Reagan] is remembered for his intelligence and forceful personality, but also as being somewhat cold— a young man who used humor to belittle, whose teasing was not good-natured. One of his old Eureka frat brothers, William McClellan, remembers that Moon's "needling manner . . . could bring Dutch to tears." As late as their college years, my father's brother could make him cry. I'm not sure Dad ever fully recovered from or forgave those taunts.

—Ron Reagan, on the relationship between his father and his uncle Neil, from *My Father at 100* by Ron Reagan

Going to college offered me the chance to play football for four more years.

—*An American Life: The Autobiography* by Ronald Reagan

In my first year and a half at Warner Brothers, I made thirteen pictures. Usually, I was in and out of a movie in three or four weeks. You worked from eight in the morning until seven at night.

—*An American Life: The Autobiography* by Ronald Reagan

I was proud of some of the B pictures we made, but a lot of them were pretty poor. They were movies the studio didn't want good, they wanted 'em Thursday.

—*An American Life: The Autobiography* by Ronald Reagan

So much of our profession is taken up with pretending, with the interpretation of never-never roles, that an actor must spend at least half his waking hours in fantasy, in rehearsal or shooting. If he is only an actor, I feel, he is much like I was in *Kings Row,* only half a man—no matter how great his talents.

—*Where's the Rest of Me?* by Ronald Reagan with Richard G. Hubler

In Hollywood, if you didn't sing or dance, you would end up
as an after-dinner speaker, so they made me an
after-dinner speaker.

—Remark quoted in *REAGAN THE MAN, THE PRESIDENT* by Hedrick Smith,
Adam Clymer, Leonard Silk, Robert Lindsey, and Richard Burt

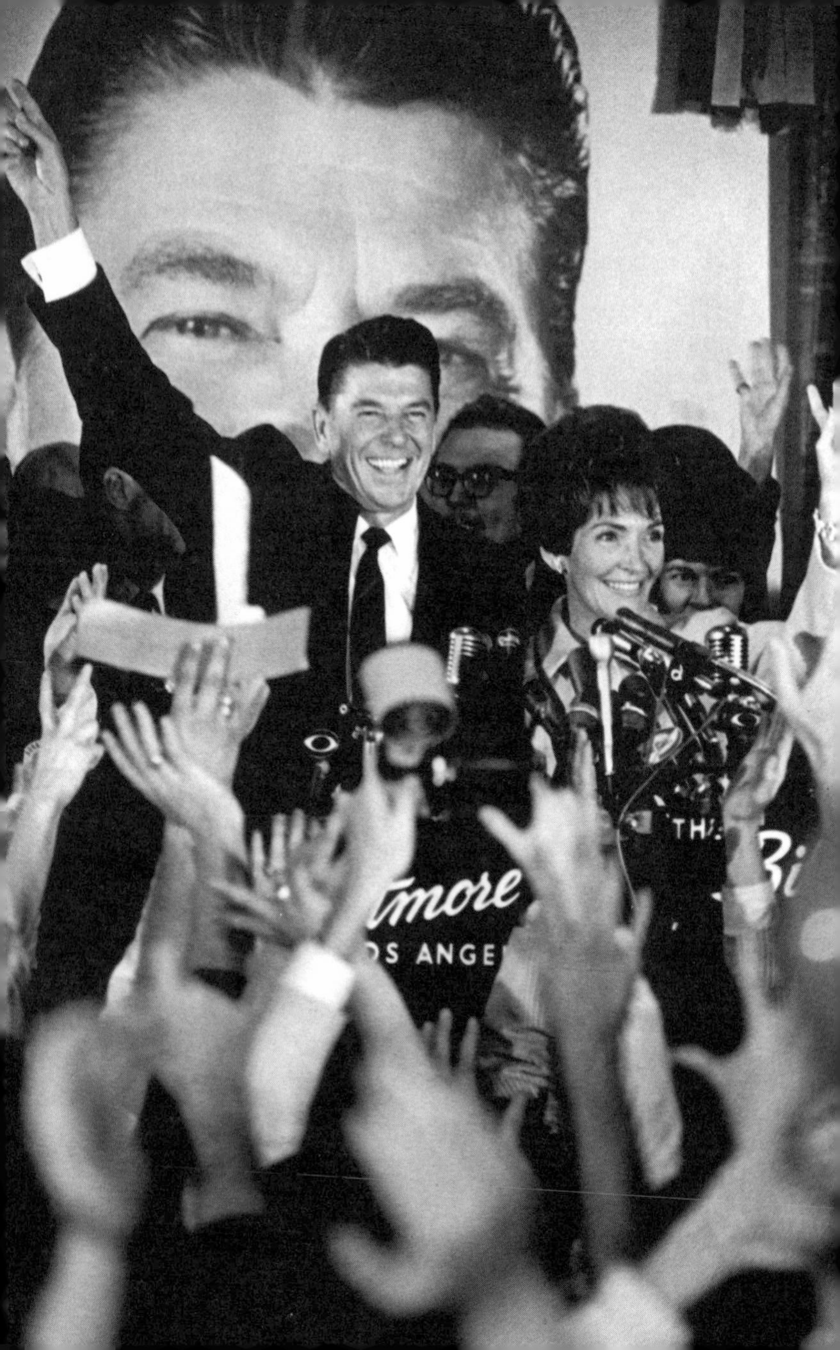
tmore
OS ANGE

DEMOCRACY
AND GOVERNMENT

Democracy is worth dying for, because it's the most deeply honorable form of government ever devised by man.

—Remarks at a ceremony commemorating the 40th anniversary of D-Day, June 6, 1984, Normandy, France

Good citizenship is vitally important if democracy is to survive and flourish. It means keeping abreast of the important issues of the day and knowing the stakes involved in the great conflicts of our time. It means bearing arms when necessary to fight for your country, for right, and for freedom. Good citizenship and defending democracy means living up to the ideals and values that make this country great. Today the world looks to America for leadership. They look to what they call our miracle economy for an answer to how they may give their people a better life. And they look to our courage and might to protect them from the forces of tyranny, brutality, and injustice.

—Address to Marine Corps basic training graduates, Parris Island, South Carolina, June 4, 1986

I consider it a tragedy that at some campuses in my own country, those who hold unfashionable ideas are hooted off the stage, or denied a forum in the first place. What a travesty on intellectual inquiry; what a perversion of the great chaotic, yet essential marketplace of ideas that we call democracy. But then, I have always believed, at home and abroad, that the only cure for what ails democracy is more democracy.

—Remarks to the Oxford Union Society, Oxford, England, December 4, 1992

The top priority of the federal government is the safety of this country.

—Address to a joint session of the Oklahoma State Legislature, March 16, 1982

By 1960, I realized that the real enemy wasn't big business, it was big government.

—*An American Life: The Autobiography* by Ronald Reagan

We always must ask: Is government working to liberate and empower the individual? Is it creating incentives for people to produce, save, invest, and profit from legitimate risks and honest toil? Is it encouraging all of us to reach for the stars? Or does it seek to compel, command, and coerce people into submission and dependence? Ask these questions, because no matter where you look today, you will see that development depends on economic freedom.

—Address to the World Affairs Council of Philadelphia, October 15, 1981

∾

I can't help thinking that, while much of the 20th century saw the rise of the federal government, the 21st century will be the century of the states. I have always believed that America is strongest and freest and happiest when it is truest to the wisdom of its founders.

—Remarks at the annual meeting of the National Governors Association, Cincinnati, Ohio, August 8, 1988

∾

Government has an inborn tendency to grow. And, left to itself, it will grow beyond the control of the people. Only constant complaint by the people will inhibit its growth.

—Address to the Comstock Club, Sacramento, California, August 6, 1973

No government ever voluntarily reduces itself in size.
Government programs, once launched, never disappear.
Actually, a government bureau is the nearest thing to
eternal life we'll ever see on this earth!

—Speech known as "A Time for Choosing," which Reagan delivered
at rallies and at the Republican National Convention in support
of Barry Goldwater's bid for the presidency; it aired on
October 27, 1964, and launched Reagan's political career

❧

Government is like a baby. An alimentary canal with a big
appetite at one end and no responsibility at the other.

—Remarked during his campaign for governor of California,
as quoted in *THE NEW YORK TIMES MAGAZINE*, November 1965

❧

The nine most terrifying words in the English language are,
"I'm from the government and I'm here to help."

—Remark on assistance to farmers made during a press conference,
Chicago, Illinois, August 2, 1986

❧

Government does not solve problems; it subsidizes them.

—Speech on December 11, 1972

Now, so there will be no misunderstanding, it's not my intention to do away with government. It is rather to make it work—work with us, not over us; to stand by our side, not ride on our back. Government can and must provide opportunity, not smother it; foster productivity, not stifle it.

—First inaugural address, January 20, 1981

Although I held public office for a total of sixteen years, I also thought of myself as a citizen-politician, not a career one. Every now and then when I was in government, I would remind my associates that "When we start thinking of government as 'us' instead of 'them,' we've been here too long." By that I mean that elected officeholders need to retain a certain skepticism about the perfectibility of government.

—Address to the Los Angeles Junior Chamber of Commerce, July 10, 1991

FREEDOM, EQUALITY,
LAW AND ORDER,
AND JUSTICE

With freedom goes responsibility. Sir Winston Churchill once said you can have 10,000 regulations and still not have respect for the law. We might start with the Ten Commandments. If we lived by the Golden Rule, there would be no need for other laws.

—Speech as governor of California, 1973

Freedom is a fragile thing and is never more than one generation away from extinction. It is not ours by inheritance; it must be fought for and defended constantly by each generation, for it comes only once to a people. Those who have known freedom and then lost it have never known it again.

—Speech as governor of California, January 5, 1967

If we look to the answer as to why for so many years we achieved so much, prospered as no other people on earth, it was because here in this land we unleashed the energy and individual genius of man to a greater extent than has ever been done before. Freedom and the dignity of the individual have been more available and assured here than in any other place on earth. The price for this freedom at times has been high, but we have never been unwilling to pay the price.

—First inaugural address, January 20, 1981

To those neighbors and allies who share our freedom, we will strengthen our historic ties and assure them of our support and firm commitment. We will match loyalty with loyalty. We will strive for mutually beneficial relations. We will not use our friendship to impose on their sovereignty, for our own sovereignty is not for sale. As for the enemies of freedom, those who are potential adversaries, they will be reminded that peace is the highest aspiration of the American people. We will negotiate for it, sacrifice for it; we will never surrender for it, now or ever.

—First inaugural address, January 20, 1981

If America is to remain what God in His wisdom intended for it to be—a refuge, a safe haven for those seeking human rights—then we must once again extend the most basic human right to the most vulnerable members of the human family. We must commit ourselves to a future in which the right to life for every human being—no matter how weak, no matter how small, no matter how defenseless— is protected by our laws and public policy.

—Proclamation for National Sanctity of Human Life Day, January 14, 1985

I've always believed a free press is as vital to America as the Constitution and the Bill of Rights. A probing, responsible press not only keeps the public informed about what's going on in government, it can keep a watchful eye out to uncover corruption, waste, or mismanagement.

—*AN AMERICAN LIFE: THE AUTOBIOGRAPHY* by Ronald Reagan

With regard to the freedom of the individual for choice with regard to abortion, there's one individual who's not being considered at all. That's the one who is being aborted. And I've noticed that everybody that is for abortion has already been born.

—Remarked during the presidential debate between Ronald Reagan and John Anderson, Baltimore, Maryland, September 21, 1980

We don't lump people by groups or special interests. And let me add, in the party of Lincoln there is no room for intolerance and not even a small corner for anti-Semitism or bigotry of any kind. Many people are welcome in our house, but not the bigots.

—Speech accepting the Republican presidential nomination, Republican National Convention, Dallas, Texas, August 23, 1984

Presidents come and go. History comes and goes, but principles endure and insure future generations to defend liberty—not a gift from government, but a blessing from our Creator. Here, the lamp of individual conscience burns bright. By that I know we will all be guided to that dreamed-of day when no one wields a sword and no one drags a chain.

—Address to recipients of the Presidential Medal of Freedom, the White House, January 13, 1993

Abraham Lincoln freed the black man. In many ways, Dr. King freed the white man. How did he accomplish this tremendous feat? Where others—white and black—preached hatred, he taught the principles of love and nonviolence. We can be so thankful that Dr. King raised his mighty eloquence for love and hope rather than for hostility and bitterness. He took the tension he found in our nation, a tension of injustice, and channeled it for the good of America and all her people.

—Address on the anniversary of the birth of Martin Luther King, Jr., the White House, January 15, 1983

We spoke for an hour or so upstairs in the family quarters, and I literally told him my life story—how Jack and Nelle had raised me from the time I was a child to believe racial and religious discrimination was the worst sin in the world, how I'd experienced some of it as the son of an Irish Catholic in a Protestant town; how as a sports announcer I'd been among the first in the country to campaign for integration of professional baseball; how I'd tried as governor to open up opportunities for blacks. That night, I think I made a friend.

—Reagan recalling his meeting with Supreme Court Justice Thurgood Marshall in 1987, after Marshall had implied in a televised interview that Reagan was a racist, from *An American Life: The Autobiography* by Ronald Reagan

I was never able to convince many black citizens of my commitment to their needs. They often mistook my belief in keeping the government out of the average American's life as a cover for doing nothing about racial injustice. I think of all things that were said about me during my presidency, this charge bothers me the most personally. I abhor racism. These skinheads and white supremacist groups have no place in this country. They are not what we are about, and I wish they would just vaporize.

—*Speaking My Mind: Selected Speeches* by Ronald Reagan

We must reject the idea that every time a law's broken,
society is guilty rather than the lawbreaker. It is time to
restore the American precept that each individual
is accountable for his actions.

—Speech at the Republican National Convention, Miami Beach, Florida,
August 1968

∽

One legislator accused me of having a nineteenth-century
attitude on law and order. That is a totally false charge.
I have an eighteenth-century attitude. That is when
the Founding Fathers made it clear that the safety
of law-abiding citizens should be one of the
government's primary concerns.

—Address to the Republican State Central Committee Convention,
San Diego, California, September 7, 1973

∽

The crime problem has indeed become a matter of widespread
concern, even among people of different philosophies.
Today's hard-liner on law and order is yesterday's liberal
who was mugged last night.

—Speech as governor of California, August 1, 1973

I mean no irreverence when I mention that I once played a sheriff on TV who thought he could do the job without a gun. I was dead in the first 27 minutes of the show.

—Remarks at the annual meeting of the International Association of Chiefs of Police, New Orleans, Louisiana, September 28, 1981

❧

You won't get gun control by disarming law-abiding citizens. There's only one way to get real gun control: Disarm the thugs and the criminals, lock them up, and if you don't actually throw away the key, at least lose it for a long time.

—Remarks at the "Salute to the President Dinner," Long Beach, California, June 30, 1983

❧

With the right to bear arms comes a great responsibility to use caution and common sense on handgun purchases. And it's just plain common sense that there be a waiting period to allow local law-enforcement officials to conduct background checks on those who wish to buy a handgun.

—Speech at the George Washington University Convocation, Washington, D.C., March 28, 1991

I have never given a litmus test to anyone that I have
appointed to the bench. . . . I feel very strongly about
those social issues, but I also place my confidence in the
fact that the one thing that I do seek are judges that will
interpret the law and not write the law. We've had too many
examples in recent years of courts and judges legislating.
They're not interpreting what the law says and whether
someone has violated it or not. In too many instances,
they have been actually legislating by legal decree
what they think the law should be, and that I don't go for.
And I think that the two men that we're just talking about
here, Rehnquist and Scalia, are interpreters of
the Constitution and the law.

—Interview with the *Los Angeles Times*, June 23, 1986

I believe the American people will reject the politicization
of our judiciary. When the people begin to hear the truth,
they will demand an independent judiciary, free from
high-pressure politics and founded on the principle
of judicial restraint.

—Remarks at the Republican Governors Club Annual Dinner,
Washington, D.C., October 15, 1987

Each new generation of Americans inherits as a birthright the legal protections secured, protected, and expanded by the vigilance of preceding generations. These rights—freedom of speech, trial by jury, personal liberty, a representative and limited government, and equal protection of the laws, to name but a few—give every citizen a vested interest in American justice.

—**Proclamation for Law Day U.S.A., April 15, 1983**

AMERICA

I, in my own mind, have always thought of America as a place in the divine scheme of things that was set aside as a promised land. It was set here and the price of admission was very simple: the means of selection was very simple as to how this land should be populated. Any place in the world and any person from those places; any person with the courage, with the desire to tear up their roots, to strive for freedom, to attempt and dare to live in a strange and foreign place, to travel halfway across the world was welcome here.

—Commencement address at William Woods College, Fulton, Missouri, June 2, 1952

It is time for us to realize that we're too great a nation to limit ourselves to small dreams. We're not, as some would have us believe, doomed to an inevitable decline. I do not believe in a fate that will fall on us no matter what we do. I do believe in a fate that will fall on us if we do nothing. So, with all the creative energy at our command, let us begin an era of national renewal. Let us renew our determination, our courage, and our strength. And let us renew our faith and our hope. We have every right to dream heroic dreams. Those who say that we're in a time when there are no heroes, they just don't know where to look.

—First inaugural address, January 20, 1981

There is, in America, a greatness and a tremendous heritage
of idealism, which is a reservoir of strength and goodness.
It is ours if we will but tap it. And because of this—because
that greatness is there—there is need in America today
for a reaffirmation of that goodness and a re-formation
of our greatness.

—Speech at the Conservative Political Action Conference,
Washington, D.C., March 20, 1981

∾

I hope the people on Wall Street will pay attention to the
people on Main Street. If they do, they will see there is a
rising tide of confidence in the future of America.

—Remarked in summer 1981

∾

A President's greatest responsibility is to protect all our
people from enemies, foreign and domestic. Here at home
the worst enemy we face is economic—the creeping erosion
of the American way of life and the American dream that
has resulted in today's tragedy of economic stagnation
and unemployment.

—Address to the nation on the economy, October 13, 1982

An America that is militarily and economically strong is not enough. The world must see an America that is morally strong with a creed and a vision. This is what has led us to dare and achieve. For us, values count.

—Remarks at the annual convention of the Congressional Medal of Honor Society, New York City, December 12, 1983

⁓

We've been blessed with the opportunity to stand for something—for liberty and freedom and fairness. And these are things worth fighting for, worth devoting our lives to.

—Remarks at the Conservative Political Action Conference, Washington, D.C., March 1, 1985

⁓

America represents something universal in the human spirit. I received a letter not long ago from a man who said, "You can go to Japan to live, but you cannot become Japanese. You can go to France to live and not become a Frenchman. You can go to live in Germany or Turkey, and you won't become a German or a Turk." But then he added, "Anybody from any corner of the world can come to America to live and become an American."

—Speech at a presidential campaign rally for George Bush, San Diego, California, November 7, 1988

We keep adding new Americans all the time . . . and the
diversity of their backgrounds makes us all richer. I'll confess
to getting a lump in my throat when I witnessed
a swearing-in ceremony for new citizens. Written on their
faces was happiness, pride and determination to pursue
their vision of the American dream.

—Address to the Los Angeles Junior Chamber of Commerce,
July 10, 1991

And let me offer lesson number one about America: All great
change in America begins at the dinner table.

—Farewell address to the nation, January 11, 1989

I believe we, the Americans of today, are ready to act worthy
of ourselves, ready to do what must be done to ensure
happiness and liberty for ourselves, our children, and our
children's children. And as we renew ourselves here in
our own land, we will be seen as having greater strength
throughout the world. We will again be the exemplar
of freedom and a beacon of hope for those who
do not now have freedom.

—First inaugural address, January 20, 1981

The poet called Miss Liberty's torch "the lamp beside the golden door." Well, that was the entrance to America, and it still is. And now you really know why we're here tonight. The glistening hope of that lamp is still ours. Every promise, every opportunity, is still golden in this land. And through that golden door our children can walk into tomorrow with the knowledge that no one can be denied the promise that is America. Her heart is full; her torch is still golden, her future bright. She has arms big enough to comfort and strong enough to support, for the strength in her arms is the strength of her people. She will carry on in the '80s unafraid, unashamed, and unsurpassed. In this springtime of hope, some lights seem eternal; America's is.

—Speech accepting the Republican presidential nomination,
Republican National Convention, Dallas, Texas, August 23, 1984

Some may try and tell us that this is the end of an era. But what they overlook is that in America every day is a new beginning, and every sunset is merely the latest milestone on a voyage that never ends. For this is the land that has never become, but is always in the act of becoming. Emerson was right: America is the Land of Tomorrow.

—Speech accepting the Presidential Medal of Freedom,
the White House, January 13, 1993

POLITICS

I had been lauded as a star in sports and had been praised in movies: in politics I found myself misrepresented, cursed, vilified, denounced, and libeled. Yet it was by far the most fascinating part of my life.

—*WHERE'S THE REST OF ME?* by Ronald Reagan with Richard G. Hubler

❧

Those GE tours became almost a postgraduate course in political science for me. I was seeing how government really operated and affected people in America, not how it was taught in school. From hundreds of people in every part of the country, I heard complaints about how the ever-expanding federal government was encroaching on liberties we'd always taken for granted.

—*AN AMERICAN LIFE: THE AUTOBIOGRAPHY* by Ronald Reagan

❧

Having been a Democrat most of my life, I know how hard it is to mark that ballot the other way. It's almost like changing religions.

—Remarked in 1978

I know what it's like to pull the Republican lever for the first time, because I used to be a Democrat myself, and I can tell you it only hurts for a minute and then it feels just great.

—Remarks at a campaign appearance, Bayonne, New Jersey,
October 25, 1980

∾

This is the issue of this election: whether we believe in our capacity for self-government or whether we abandon the American Revolution and confess that a little intellectual elite in a far-distant capital can plan our lives for us better than we can plan them ourselves.

—Speech known as "A Time for Choosing," in support of
Barry Goldwater, October 27, 1964

∾

We've heard a great deal about Republican fat cats—how the Republicans are the party of big contributions. I've never been able to understand why a Republican contributor is a fat cat and a Democratic contributor of the same amount of money is a public-spirited philanthropist.

—Remarks at a Republican fund-raiser, Los Angeles, California,
August 4, 1974

I didn't know whether I'd been elected governor or appointed receiver.

—Remark about California's financial woes at the time of his election, March 31, 1976

❧

Politics is just like show business. You have a hell of an opening, coast for a while, and then have a hell of a close.

—Remark to Stuart Spencer, 1966

❧

For many years now, you and I have been shushed like children and told there are no simple answers to the complex problems that are beyond our comprehension. Well, the truth is there are simple answers. There are just not easy ones.

—Inaugural address as governor of California, January 1967

❧

I sometimes wonder what the Ten Commandments would have looked like if Moses had to run them through a Democratic legislature.

—Remark as governor of California, 1969

Sadly I have come to realize that a great many so-called liberals aren't liberal—they will defend to the death your right to agree with them.

—*WHERE'S THE REST OF ME?* by Ronald Reagan with Richard G. Hubler

∾

When you can't make them see the light, make them feel the heat.

—Attributed

∾

I have learned that one of the most important rules in politics is poise—which means looking like an owl after you have behaved like a jackass.

—Remarks at a legislative luncheon, Sacramento, California, August 9, 1973

∾

There are some days you go home so frustrated that you get in the shower and you make speeches to the walls of the shower. But there are other days when you go home and feel ten feet tall because you have solved a problem.

—Remark as governor of California, May 1, 1973

I am paying for this microphone!

—Remarked during a debate for the Republican presidential nomination in 1980 when the moderator ordered Reagan's microphone turned off after Reagan asked for the participation of the other candidates

∽

I don't pay much attention to critics. The world is divided into two kinds of people: those who can, and those who criticize.

—Remark quoted in "Prompting the President" by Michael Korda in *The New Yorker*, October 6, 1997

∽

Dear Sam:

I'm delighted that you are staying on the White House beat. I hope you won't be so self-effacing, quiet and shy as you have been in the past. Speak right up when you have a question.

Your compassionate master,
Ronald Reagan

P.S. I've worn a brand-new suit twice and you haven't noticed or asked me about it.

—Letter to Sam Donaldson, December 20, 1984, *Dear Americans: Letters from the Desk of Ronald Reagan* edited by Ralph E. Weber and Ralph A. Weber

I think the fact of our friendship is testimony to the political
system that we're part of, and the country we live in;
a country which permits two not-so-shy and not-so-retiring
Irishmen to have it out on the issues, rather than on
each other or their countrymen.

—Remarks at a dinner honoring Tip O'Neill, Washington, D.C.,
March 17, 1986

When you see all that rhetorical smoke billowing up from
the Democrats . . . well, ladies and gentlemen, I'd follow the
example of their nominee: don't inhale.

—Remarks at the Republican National Convention, Houston, Texas,
August 17, 1992

Well, at this point in my career, I'm used to a certain amount
of skepticism. Back in 1966, when somebody told my
old boss, Jack Warner, that I was running for governor of
California, he thought for a minute and said, "No, Jimmy
Stewart for governor, Reagan for best friend."

—Remarks at a White House briefing on the Economic Bill of Rights,
July 22, 1987

Politics is supposed to be the second oldest profession.
I have come to realize that it bears a very close resemblance
to the first. I'm convinced that today the majority of
Americans want what those first Americans wanted:
a better life for themselves and their children; a minimum
of government authority. Very simply, they want to be left
alone in peace and safety to take care of the family by earning
an honest dollar and putting away some savings. This may
not sound too exciting, but there is something magnificent
about it. On the farm, on the street corner, in the factory,
and in the kitchen, millions of us ask nothing more,
but certainly nothing less, than to live our own lives
according to our values—at peace with ourselves,
our neighbors, and the world.

—Address to the nation marking the bicentennial, July 6, 1976

According to the experts, I have exceeded my life expectancy
by quite a few years. Now this is a source of great annoyance
to some, especially those in the Democratic Party.

—Remarks at the Republican National Convention, Houston, Texas,
August 17, 1992

THE PRESIDENCY

A troubled and afflicted mankind looks to us, pleading for us to keep our rendezvous with destiny; that we will uphold the principles of self-reliance, self-discipline, morality, and above all, responsible liberty for every individual that we will become that shining city on a hill. They tell us we must learn to live with less, and teach our children that their lives will be less full and prosperous than ours have been; that the America of the coming years will be a place where—because of our past excesses—it will be impossible to dream and make those dreams come true. I don't believe that. And I don't believe you do, either. That is why I am seeking the presidency.

—Announcement of candidacy for U.S. president, November 13, 1979

More than anything else, I want my candidacy to unify our country, to renew the American spirit and sense of purpose. I want to carry our message to every American, regardless of party affiliation, who is a member of the community of shared values.

—Speech accepting the Republican presidential nomination, Republican National Convention, July 17, 1980, Detroit, Michigan

We now know what Mr. Carter plans to do with four more years. Catch your breath, hold on to your hats, and grab your wallets because Jimmy Carter's analysis of the economy means that his answer is higher taxes.

—Campaign speech in Lima, Ohio, October 15, 1980

❦

Next Tuesday all of you will go to the polls, will stand there in the polling place and make a decision. I think when you make that decision it might be well if you would ask yourself: Are you better off than you were four years ago?

—Remarked during a televised presidential debate between Ronald Reagan and Jimmy Carter, Cleveland, Ohio, October 28, 1980

❦

There you go again!

—Remark to Jimmy Carter during a 1980 presidential debate in which Carter argued that Reagan was opposed to Medicare

❦

No matter how much [Carter] tries to run away from his record, he has to account for it to the American people.

—Campaign speech in Des Plaines, Illinois, October 31, 1980

To a few of us here today this is a solemn and most momentous occasion, and yet in the history of our nation it is a commonplace occurrence. The orderly transfer of authority as called for in the Constitution routinely takes place, as it has for almost two centuries, and few of us stop to think how unique we really are. In the eyes of many in the world, this every-four-year ceremony we accept as normal is nothing less than a miracle.

—First inaugural address, January 20, 1981

It is my intention to curb the size and influence of the federal establishment and to demand recognition of the distinction between the powers granted to the federal government and those reserved to the states or to the people. All of us need to be reminded that the federal government did not create the states; the states created the federal government.

—First inaugural address, January 20, 1981

It is not my intention to do away with government. It is rather to make it work—work with us, not over us; stand by our side, not ride on our back. Government can and must provide opportunity, not smother it; foster productivity, not stifle it. This administration's objective will be a healthy, vigorous, growing economy.

—First inaugural address, January 20, 1981

In the days ahead I will propose removing the roadblocks that have slowed our economy and reduced productivity. Steps will be taken aimed at restoring the balance between the various levels of government. Progress may be slow, measured in inches and feet, not miles, but we will progress. It is time to reawaken this industrial giant, to get government back within its means, and to lighten our punitive tax burden. And these will be our first priorities, and on these principles there will be no compromise.

—First inaugural address, January 20, 1981

Before going to my first economic summit, I'd wondered what it would be like to have the heads of seven nations in the same room: What tensions of ego and status would be at work? . . . But, as our first meeting got started, I was surprised to hear the others addressing each other by their first names. When I got my first chance to speak, I said, "My name's Ron. . ." Although I never asked her about it, I think the idea of addressing the other summit leaders by their first names was Margaret Thatcher's. It did wonders to make the meetings cordial and productive. I was always Ron to the others and I addressed them by their first names.

—*An American Life: The Autobiography* by Ronald Reagan

We'll all do the job as if there will never be another
election. In other words . . . we'll take no actions or make
no decisions that are based on how they might bear on
or affect an election. Whatever we do will be based on
what we believe, to the best of our ability, is best for
the people of this country.

—Reagan's remarks at his first cabinet meeting, March 30, 1981, quoted
in *THE REAGAN REVOLUTION* by Rowland Evans and Robert Novak

A busy hectic day—but the Senate voted cloture & then
passed the gas tax highway bill. Thank Heaven the Congress
has now gone home.

Final meeting with King Hussein. I believe we've
made great progress and, unless the Israelis throw sand in
the gears, he should be back here in a few weeks to announce
he'll negotiate with them.

A full day of meetings on Federalism, Women's issues,
the Private Initiative program, etc.

—Excerpt from Reagan's diary, December 23, 1982,
THE REAGAN DIARIES edited by Douglas Brinkley

We should also answer the question of public service: Why
are we here? What do we believe in? Well for one thing,
we're here to see that government continues to serve
the people and not the other way around. Yes, government
should do all that is necessary, but only that
which is necessary.

—Speech accepting the Republican presidential nomination,
Republican National Convention, Dallas, Texas, August 23, 1984

෴

This is not the end of anything. This is the beginning
of everything.

—Remark quoted in *TIME*, November 1984, on his reelection

෴

We will never forget them, nor the last time we saw them
this morning, as they prepared for the journey and waved
goodbye and "slipped the surly bonds of earth" to
"touch the face of God."

—Speech after the loss of the space shuttle *CHALLENGER* and
all of its crew, the White House, January 28, 1986

Surround yourself with the best people you can find,
delegate authority, and don't interfere.

—Interview in *FORTUNE* magazine describing his management style,
September 15, 1986

The best you can do is try to get the best advice you can,
listen carefully to many different views, make your decision
and implement it with care, and keep testing your judgment
to see if you need to make adjustments.

—Interview with representatives of *LE FIGARO*, December 22, 1983

Much has been said about my management style, a style
that's worked successfully for me during eight years as
governor of California and for most of my presidency.
The way I work is to identify the problem, find the right
individuals to do the job, and then let them go to it.
I've found this invariably brings out the best in people.
They seem to rise to their full capability, and
in the long run you get more done.

—Address to the nation on the Iran–Contra scandal, March 4, 1987

First, let me say I take full responsibility for my own actions
and for those of my administration. As angry as I may be
about activities undertaken without my knowledge, I am
still accountable for those activities. As disappointed as
I may be in some who served me, I'm still the one who
must answer to the American people for this behavior.
And as personally distasteful as I find secret bank accounts
and diverted funds—well, as the Navy would say,
this happened on my watch.

—Address to the nation on the Iran–Contra scandal, March 4, 1987

A few months ago I told the American people I did not trade
arms for hostages. My heart and my best intentions still tell
me that's true, but the facts and the evidence tell me it is
not. As the Tower board reported, what began as a strategic
opening to Iran deteriorated, in its implementation, into
trading arms for hostages. This runs counter to my own
beliefs, to administration policy, and to the original strategy
we had in mind. There are reasons why it happened, but
no excuses. It was a mistake. I undertook the original Iran
initiative in order to develop relations with those who might
assume leadership in a post-Khomeini government.

—Address to the nation on the Iran–Contra scandal, March 4, 1987

The 7th & best St. of the U. I've never had such a reception with even the Dem's. clapping. I was interrupted 37 times by applause. The speech ran 43 min's. because of it. I surprised Nancy by singling her out in the gallery & praising her for her anti-drug activity.

—Excerpt from Reagan's diary, January 25, 1988,
THE REAGAN DIARIES edited by Douglas Brinkley

On an average day when I was president, I saw about eighty people, ranging from presidents and prime ministers to the newest multiple sclerosis poster child. Some days, there were more than twenty appointments on my schedule, from about nine in the morning until at least five in the afternoon. . . . You get introduced to hundreds of people, hear their names only once, and don't always put together a name with a face in a moment's time.

—*AN AMERICAN LIFE: THE AUTOBIOGRAPHY* by Ronald Reagan

This was an especially emotional time for Nancy and me. For eight years, the White House had been our home. From around the nation, members of the White House staff and others in the administration had come to Washington to be part of our team, and we had become like a family. Now it was time to move on and we all felt sadness about it.

—*An American Life: The Autobiography* by **Ronald Reagan**

One of the things about the presidency is that you're always somewhat apart. You spend a lot of time going by too fast in a car someone else is driving and seeing the people through tinted glass—the parents holding up a child and the wave you saw too late and couldn't return. And so many times I wanted to stop and reach out from behind the glass and connect.

—**Farewell address to the nation, January 11, 1989**

It's been the honor of my life to be your president. So many of you have written the past few weeks to say thanks, but I could say as much for you. Nancy and I are grateful for the opportunity you gave us to serve.

—**Farewell address to the nation, January 11, 1989**

I won a nickname, "The Great Communicator." But I never thought it was my style or the words I used that made a difference: It was the content. I wasn't a great communicator, but I communicated great things, and they didn't spring full bloom from my brow, they came from the heart of a great nation—from our experience, our wisdom, and our belief in principles that have guided us for two centuries. They called it the Reagan revolution. Well, I'll accept that, but for me it always seemed more like the great rediscovery, a rediscovery of our values and our common sense.

—Farewell address to the nation, January 11, 1989

I've spoken of the shining city all my political life, but I don't know if I ever quite communicated what I saw when I said it. . . . In my mind it was a tall, proud city built on rocks stronger than oceans, windswept, God-blessed, and teeming with people of all kinds living in harmony and peace; a city with free ports that hummed with commerce and creativity. And if there had to be city walls, the walls had doors and the doors were open to anyone with the will and the heart to get there. That's how I saw it, and see it still.

—Farewell address to the nation, January 11, 1989

We've done our part. And as I walk off into the city streets, a final word to the men and women of the Reagan revolution, the men and women across America who for eight years did the work that brought America back. My friends: We did it. We weren't just marking time. We made a difference. We made the city stronger. We made the city freer, and we left her in good hands. All in all, not bad, not bad at all. And so, good-bye, God bless you, and God bless the United States of America.

—Farewell address to the nation, January 11, 1989

Our friends in the other party will never forgive us for our success and are doing everything in their power to rewrite history. Listening to the liberals, you'd think that the 1980s were the worst period since the Great Depression, filled with suffering and despair. I don't know about you, but I'm getting awfully tired of the whining voices from the White House these days. They're claiming there was a decade of greed and neglect, but you and I know better than that. We were there.

—Remarks at the Republican National Convention Annual Gala, February 3, 1994

PEACE, WAR,
THE MILITARY, AND
FOREIGN POLICY

I believe with all my heart that our first priority must be world peace, and that use of force is always and only a last resort, when everything else has failed, and then only with regard to our national security.

—Remarks at a ceremony commemorating the 40th anniversary of D-Day, June 6, 1984, Normandy, France

Peace is not the absence of conflict, but the ability to cope with conflict by peaceful means.

—Commencement address at Eureka College, Eureka, Illinois, May 9, 1982

When we speak of peace, we should not mean just the absence of war. True peace rests on the pillars of individual freedom, human rights, national self-determination, and respect for the rule of law.

—Address to the nation prior to the U.S.–Soviet summit in Geneva, November 14, 1985

A people free to choose will always choose peace.

—Address at Moscow State University, May 31, 1988

We in America have learned bitter lessons from two world wars: it is better to be here, ready to protect the peace, than to take blind shelter across the sea, rushing to respond only after freedom is lost. We've learned that isolationism never was and never will be an acceptable response to tyrannical governments with an expansionist intent.

—Remarks at a ceremony commemorating the 40th anniversary of D-Day, June 6, 1984, Normandy, France

Above all, we must realize that no arsenal or no weapon in the arsenals of the world is so formidable as the will and moral courage of free men and women. It is a weapon our adversaries in today's world do not have. It is a weapon that we as Americans do have. Let that be understood by those who practice terrorism and prey upon their neighbors.

—First inaugural address, January 20, 1981

We're in greater danger today than we were the day after Pearl Harbor. Our military is absolutely incapable of defending this country.

—Remark quoted in *New York Magazine*, June 22, 1981

To blame the military for war makes about as much sense as suggesting that we get rid of cancer by getting rid of doctors.

—Speech at the University of California, Los Angeles, June 7, 1970

None of the four wars in my lifetime came about because we were too strong. It is weakness that invites adventurous adversaries to make mistaken judgments. America is the most peaceful, least warlike nation in modern history. We are not the cause of all the ills of the world. We're a patient and generous people. But for the sake of our freedom and that of others, we cannot permit our reserve to be confused with a lack of resolve.

—Speech accepting the Republican presidential nomination, Republican National Convention, Dallas, Texas, August 23, 1984

If we are forced to fight, we must have the means and the determination to prevail or we will not have what it takes to secure the peace.

—Remark quoted in *REAGAN THE MAN, THE PRESIDENT* by Hedrick Smith, Adam Clymer, Leonard Silk, Robert Lindsey, and Richard Burt

A truly successful army is one that, because of its strength
and ability and dedication, will not be called upon to fight,
for no one will dare to provoke it.

—Address at the United States Military Academy, West Point, New York,
May 27, 1981

❧

You use whatever force is necessary to achieve the purpose,
and I would like to feel that there wouldn't be a need
for using armed force if we made it apparent that
we have the will, if necessary, to do that.

—Remark quoted in REAGAN THE MAN, THE PRESIDENT by Hedrick Smith,
Adam Clymer, Leonard Silk, Robert Lindsey, and Richard Burt

❧

When we've taken up arms, it has been for the defense of
freedom for ourselves and for other peaceful nations who
needed our help. But now, faced with the development of
weapons of immense destructive power, we have no choice
but to maintain ready defense forces that are second to none.
Yes, the cost is high, but the price of neglect
would be infinitely higher.

—Remarks at the recommissioning of the USS *New Jersey*,
December 28, 1982

Perhaps at this late date, we can all agree that we've learned one lesson: that young Americans must never again be sent to fight and die unless we are prepared to let them win.

—Remarks at a Veterans Day ceremony at the Vietnam Veterans Memorial, Washington, D.C., November 11, 1988

❧

The defense policy of the United States is based on a simple premise: The United States does not start fights. We will never be an aggressor. We maintain our strength in order to deter and defend against aggression—to preserve freedom and peace.

—Address to the nation on defense and national security, known as the "Star Wars" speech, March 23, 1983

❧

I call upon the scientific community in our country, those who gave us nuclear weapons, to turn their great talents now to the cause of mankind and world peace, to give us the means of rendering those nuclear weapons impotent and obsolete.

—Address to the nation on defense and national security, known as the "Star Wars" speech, March 23, 1983

What if free people could live secure in the knowledge that
their security did not rest upon the threat of instant U.S.
retaliation to deter a Soviet attack, that we could intercept
and destroy strategic ballistic missiles before they reached
our own soil or that of our allies? I know this is a formidable,
technical task, one that may not be accomplished before the
end of this century. Yet, current technology has attained a
level of sophistication where it's reasonable for us to begin
this effort. It will take years, probably decades of effort on
many fronts. There will be failures and setbacks, just as there
will be successes and breakthroughs. And as we proceed,
we must remain constant in preserving the nuclear deterrent
and maintaining a solid capability for flexible response.
But isn't it worth every investment necessary to free the
world from the threat of nuclear war? We know it is.

—Address to the nation on defense and national security, known as the
"Star Wars" speech, March 23, 1983

We are especially not going to tolerate these attacks from
outlaw states run by the strangest collection of misfits,
Looney Tunes, and squalid criminals since the
advent of the Third Reich.

—Speech following the hijacking of a U.S. airplane, July 8, 1985

History teaches that wars begin when governments believe the price of aggression is cheap.

—Address to the nation, January 6, 1984

Today we have done what we had to do. If necessary, we shall do it again. It gives me no pleasure to say that, and I wish it were otherwise. . . . When our citizens are abused or attacked anywhere in the world on the direct orders of a hostile regime, we will respond so long as I'm in this Oval Office. Self-defense is not only our right; it is our duty. . . . Despite our repeated warnings, Qadhafi continued his reckless policy of intimidation, his relentless pursuit of terror. He counted on America to be passive. He counted wrong.

—Address to the nation on the U.S. air strike against Libya, April 14, 1986

There is no way for America to turn inward and embrace isolationism in the world as it is today without jeopardizing all the progress we have made toward peace in this century.

—Address to the Los Angeles World Affairs Council, October 12, 1972

A nuclear war cannot be won, and must never be fought.

—Remarks from a summit on arms control, Reykjavík, Iceland, 1986

Despite the spread of democracy and capitalism, human nature has not changed. It is still an unpredictable mixture of good and evil. Our enemies may be irrational, even outright insane, driven by nationalism, religion, ethnicity, or ideology. They do not fear the United States for its diplomatic skills or the number of automobiles and software programs it produces. They respect only the firepower of our tanks, planes, and helicopter gunships.

—Commencement address at The Citadel, Charleston, South Carolina,
May 15, 1993

The challenge of statesmanship is to have the vision to dream of a better, safer world and the courage, persistence and patience to turn that dream into a reality.

—Remarks to the U.S. negotiating team for the nuclear and space arms
negotiations with the Soviet Union, Washington, D.C., March 8, 1985

We will always remember. We will always be proud. We will always be prepared, so we may always be free.

—Remarks at a ceremony commemorating the 40th anniversary of
D-Day, June 6, 1984, Normandy, France

THE ECONOMY, BUSINESS, AND LABOR

If all of this seems like a great deal of trouble, think what's at stake. We are faced with the most evil enemy mankind has known in his long climb from the swamp to the stars. There can be no security anywhere in the free world if there is no fiscal and economic stability within the United States. Those who ask us to trade our freedom for the soup kitchen of the welfare state are architects of a policy of accommodation.

—Speech known as "A Time for Choosing," in support of
Barry Goldwater, October 27, 1964

This absorption of revenue by all levels of government, the alarming rate of inflation and the rising toll of unemployment all stem from a single source: the belief that government, particularly the federal government, has the answer to our ills, and that the proper method of dealing with social problems is to transfer power from the private to the public sector, and within the public sector from state and local governments to the ultimate power center in Washington. This collectivist, centralizing approach, whatever name or party label it wears, has created our economic problems.

—Address to the Executives' Club of Chicago, September 26, 1975

I'd only been in the Oval Office a few days when I became
embroiled in a fight in which I had to persuade Congress
to raise the ceiling on the national debt. Because of the
spending excesses of the past, everyone in Washington knew
the ceiling had to be raised—otherwise, the country would
be broke and not able to pay its bills. But in an example
of the games I later learned they played all the time, many of
the Democrats tried to make it appear to the public that the
first thing the new guy in the White House wanted to do
after campaigning in favor of cutting the federal deficit was
to raise the national debt. It was another example of
the Congress flexing its muscles at the new boy in town.
With a show of great reluctance, the Democrats finally
relented and voted to raise the debt ceiling. Later, I learned
a similar scenario played out every year. . . .

—*An American Life: The Autobiography* by Ronald Reagan

This is not the time for political fun and games. This is
the time for a new beginning. I ask you now to put aside
any feelings of frustration or helplessness about our political
institutions and join me in this dramatic but responsible
plan to reduce the enormous burden of federal taxation
on you and your family.

—Address to the nation, July 27, 1981

We don't have a trillion-dollar debt because we haven't taxed enough; we have a trillion-dollar debt because we spend too much.

—Remarks at the National Association of Realtors Legislative Conference, March 29, 1982

This country now possesses the strongest credit in the world. The full consequences of a default or even the serious prospect of default by the United States are impossible to predict and awesome to contemplate. Denigration of the full faith and credit of the United States would have substantial effects on the domestic financial markets and on the value of the dollar in exchange markets. The Nation can ill afford to allow such a result. The risks, the cost, the disruptions, and the incalculable damage lead me to but one conclusion: the Senate must pass this legislation before the Congress adjourns.

—Letter to Senate Majority Leader Howard Baker calling for an increase in the public debt ceiling, November 16, 1983

Yes, deficits are a problem. I've been saying so for more than a quarter of a century now. But the problem is not the size of the deficit, it's the size of government's claim on our economy.

—Address to the nation, March 3, 1984

I have my veto pen drawn and ready for any tax increase
that Congress might even think of sending up. And
I have only one thing to say to the tax increasers.
Go ahead, make my day.

—Remarks to members of the American Business Conference,
Washington, D.C., March 13, 1985

❧

Government's view of the economy could be summed up in
a few short phrases: If it moves, tax it. If it keeps moving,
regulate it. And if it stops moving, subsidize it.

—Remarks to the White House Conference on Small Business,
August 15, 1986

❧

You know, I think the best possible social program is a job.

—Remarked in 1980

❧

Let me make our goal. . .very clear: jobs, jobs, jobs, and
more jobs. . . . Our policy has been and will continue to be:
What is good for the American workers is good for America.

—Labor Day message, September 4, 1981

A president's greatest responsibility is to protect all our people from enemies, foreign and domestic. Here at home the worst enemy we face is economic—the creeping erosion of the American way of life and the American dream that has resulted in today's tragedy of economic stagnation and unemployment.

—Address to the nation on the economy, October 13, 1982

Where energy needs conflict with environmental goals, we must strike a reasonable balance. It will do little good for someone to have all the gasoline he can use, if he has no job to drive to because the industry for which he worked is shut down by an energy or fuel shortage.

—State of the State address, Sacramento, California, January 9, 1974

Individual farmers, laborers, owners, traders and managers— they are the heart and soul of development. Trust them, because whenever they are allowed to create and build, wherever they are given a personal stake in deciding economic policies and benefiting from their success, then societies become more dynamic, prosperous, progressive and free.

—Remarks at the International Meeting on Cooperation and Development, Cancun, Mexico, October 22, 1981

I have a special reason for wanting to solve this [economic] problem in a lasting way. I was 21 and looking for work in 1932, one of the worst years of the Great Depression. And I can remember one bleak night in the thirties when my father learned on Christmas Eve that he'd lost his job. To be young in my generation was to feel that your future had been mortgaged out from under you, and that's a tragic mistake we must never allow our leaders to make again.

—Address to the nation on the economy, October 13, 1982

Any system that penalizes success and accomplishments is wrong. Any system that discourages work, discourages productivity, discourages economic progress is wrong. If, on the other hand, you reduce tax rates and allow people to spend or save more of what they earn, they'll be more industrious; they'll have more incentive to work hard, and money they earn will add fuel to the great economic machine that energizes our national progress. The result: more prosperity for all—and more revenue for government. A few economists call this principle supply-side economics. I just call it common sense.

—*An American Life: The Autobiography* by Ronald Reagan

Common sense told us that when you put a big tax
on something, the people will produce less of it.
So, we cut the people's tax rates, and the people
produced more than ever before.

—Farewell address to the nation, January 11, 1989

COMMUNISM AND THE SOVIET UNION

The years ahead will be great ones for our country, for
the cause of freedom and the spread of civilization.
The West will not contain communism, it will transcend
communism. We will not bother to denounce it.
We'll dismiss it as a sad, bizarre chapter in human history
whose last pages are even now being written.

—Speech at the University of Notre Dame, South Bend, Indiana,
May 17, 1981

It is the Soviet Union that runs against the tide of history. . . .
[It is] the march of freedom and democracy which will
leave Marxism–Leninism on the ash heap of history as it
has left other tyrannies which stifle the freedom and
muzzle the self-expression of the people.

—Address to members of the British Parliament, London, England,
June 8, 1982

I have one question for those rulers: If communism is the
wave of the future, why do you still need walls to keep people
in and armies of secret police to keep them quiet?

—Speech at a ceremony marking the annual observance of
Captive Nations Week, July 19, 1983

So, in your discussions of the nuclear freeze proposals,
I urge you to beware the temptation of pride, the temptation
of blithely declaring yourselves above it all and label both
sides equally at fault, to ignore the facts of history and the
aggressive impulses of an evil empire, to simply call the arms
race a giant misunderstanding and thereby remove yourself
from the struggle between right and wrong and good and
evil. . . . They preach the supremacy of the state, declare
its omnipotence over individual man and predict its
eventual domination of all peoples on the Earth. They are
the focus of evil in the modern world.

—Speech at the National Association of Evangelicals, Orlando, Florida,
March 8, 1983; it was Reagan's first use in a speech of the term
evil empire referring to the Soviet Union

And make no mistake about it, this attack was not just
against ourselves or the Republic of Korea. This was the
Soviet Union against the world and the moral precepts which
guide human relations among people everywhere. It was an
act of barbarism born of a society which wantonly disregards
individual rights and the value of human life and seeks
constantly to expand and dominate other nations.

—Address to the nation following the downing of a South Korean
airliner, September 5, 1983

I have openly expressed my view of the Soviet system.
I don't know why this should come as a surprise to Soviet
leaders, who have never shied from expressing their view of
our system. But this doesn't mean that we can't deal with
each other. We don't refuse to talk when the Soviets call us
imperialist aggressors and worse, or because they cling to
the fantasy of a communist triumph over democracy.
The fact that neither of us likes the other system is
no reason to refuse to talk.

—Address to the nation on U.S.–Soviet relations, January 16, 1984

I tell you from my heart that we in the United States
do not want war. We want to wipe from the face of the earth
the terrible weapons that man now has in his hands. And
I tell you, we are ready to seize that beachhead. We look for
some sign from the Soviet Union that they are willing
to move forward, that they share our desire and love for
peace, and that they will give up the ways of conquest.
There must be a changing there that will allow us to
turn our hope into action.

—Remarks at a ceremony commemorating the 40th anniversary of
D-Day, June 6, 1984, Normandy, France

There is one sign the Soviets can make that would be
unmistakable, that would advance dramatically the cause
of freedom and peace. General Secretary Gorbachev,
if you seek peace, if you seek prosperity for the Soviet Union
and Eastern Europe, if you seek liberalization, come here
to this gate! Mr. Gorbachev, open this gate! Mr. Gorbachev,
tear down this wall!

—Speech at the Brandenburg Gate, West Berlin, Germany,
June 12, 1987

Standing so near the Berlin Wall, seeing it in substance as
well as for what it symbolized, I felt an anger well up in
me, and I am sure this anger was reflected in my voice when
I said those words. I never dreamed that in less than three
years the wall would come down and a six-thousand-pound
section of it would be sent to me for my presidential library.

—*An American Life: The Autobiography* by Ronald Reagan

We have listened to the wisdom in an old Russian maxim.
And I'm sure you're familiar with it, Mr. General Secretary.
The maxim is . . . "trust, but verify."

—Remark at the signing of the Intermediate-Range Nuclear Forces
Treaty (INF) on nuclear arms limitation, December 8, 1987

Freedom is the right to question and change the established way of doing things. It is the continuous revolution of the marketplace. It is the understanding that allows us to recognize shortcomings and seek solutions.

—Address at Moscow State University, May 31, 1988

I want the . . . closeness to continue. And it will, as long as we make it clear that we will continue to act in a certain way as long as they continue to act in a helpful manner. If and when they don't, at first, pull your punches. If they persist, pull the plug.

—Farewell address to the nation, January 11, 1989

We recalled some of the things we'd said during our first meeting at Geneva about the importance of building trust between our countries and agreed that we had come a long way since then. Gorbachev said he regretted that I couldn't stay on and finish the job, and I have to admit there was a part of me that wanted to do that. But I had enormous faith in George Bush, and I knew the country was in good hands.

—Reagan recalling his farewell to Mikhail Gorbachev
at the end of his presidency, December 1988, from
AN AMERICAN LIFE: THE AUTOBIOGRAPHY by Ronald Reagan

FAMILY, FRIENDS, AND
LIFE'S PLEASURES

If my father was Catholic, my mother was Protestant. If he rebelled against the universe, she was a natural practical do-gooder. If he was Irish, she was Scots-English. If he was occasionally vulgar, she tried to raise the tone of the family. Perhaps she never understood the reason for his week-long benders once or twice a year, any more than he understood her cultural activities, but they put up with each other.

—*Where's the Rest of Me?* by Ronald Reagan with Richard G. Hubler

I learned from my father the value of hard work and ambition, and maybe a little something about telling a story. From my mother, I learned the value of prayer, how to have dreams and believe I could make them come true.

—*An American Life: The Autobiography* by Ronald Reagan

Ronnie is a great deal like his mother. Jack Reagan could be cynical, but Nelle believed that people are basically good. She used to visit patients in sanatoriums and mental hospitals and bring cookies and Bibles to prisoners. After the men were released, she often took them into her house until they found a job. Nelle never saw anything evil in another human being, and Ronnie is the same way.

—Nancy Reagan, *My Turn: The Memoirs of Nancy Reagan* by Nancy Reagan with William Novak

He was the best storyteller I've ever heard and the strongest
man of principle I've ever known. He believed in honesty
and hard work. In the darkest days of the Depression,
when they themselves could barely scrape by, no one ever
came to their door in need of a meal who Nelle sent away
empty-handed. So, now we come to the end of this
last campaign, and I just hope Nelle and Jack are looking
down on us right now and nodding their heads and
saying their kid did them proud.

—Reagan's remarks about his parents, Jack and Nelle Reagan,
at a presidential campaign rally for George Bush, San Diego, California,
November 7, 1988

I find my thoughts turning to my own mother, Nelle Reagan.
She was truly a remarkable woman—ever so strong in
her determination yet always tender, always giving of
herself to others. She never found time in her life to
complain; she was too busy living those values she sought
to impart in my brother and myself. She was the greatest
influence on my life, and as I think of her this weekend
I remember the words of Lincoln, "All that I am, or hope
to be, I owe to my mother."

—Address to the nation, Mother's Day, May 11, 1985

If ever God gave me evidence that He had a plan for me, it was the night He brought Nancy into my life. I have spent many hours of my life giving speeches and expressing my opinions. But it is almost impossible for me to express fully how deeply I love Nancy and how much she has filled my life. Sometimes, I think my life really began when I met Nancy. From the start, our marriage was like an adolescent's dream of what a marriage should be. It was rich and full from the beginning, and it has gotten more so with each passing day.

—*An American Life: The Autobiography* by Ronald Reagan

Forty years ago I entered a world of happiness. Nancy moved into my heart, filling an empty spot with her love. . . .
Coming home to her (even in sunny California), is like coming out of the cold into a warm, firelit room. When we're at home I miss her if she even steps out of the room. For four decades we have been side by side, step by step, hand in hand.

—Tribute to Nancy Reagan on their 40th wedding anniversary, March 6, 1992

What can you say about a man who on Mother's Day sends flowers to his mother-in-law with a note thanking her for making him the happiest man on Earth?

—Nancy Reagan

I know that during the day, even before this job, whatever I was doing, something would happen in a day and the first thing that would go through my mind was picturing myself telling [Nancy] about it when I got home. We talk about everything. Sometimes, we disagree on someone or their particular qualifications or something, but never very seriously. It's good to talk about it and have other input. I feel better always knowing that we're in agreement.

—Interview for the book FIRST LADY: A PORTRAIT OF NANCY REAGAN
by Chris Wallace

Because we were always being shuttled back and forth from Mother's house to Dad's ranch, we wound up spending a lot of time in the car. Dad did almost all of the shuttling, which was OK with us because he had a way of making a car ride loads of fun. Whenever I think back to the period just after the divorce, I picture Michael and me in the backseat of Dad's turquoise convertible, happily engaged in some game or story cooked up by our clever Dad.

—Maureen Reagan, FIRST FATHER, FIRST DAUGHTER: A MEMOIR
by Maureen Reagan

Ronnie is an affable and gregarious man who enjoys other people, but unlike most of us, he doesn't need them for companionship or approval. As he himself has told me, he seems to need only one other person—me.

—Nancy Reagan, *MY TURN: THE MEMOIRS OF NANCY REAGAN*
by Nancy Reagan with William Novak

When his families grew to be two families, he didn't walk away from the one to go to the other. But he became a father to both. To Patti and then Ronnie, but always to Maureen, my sister, and myself. We looked forward to those Saturday mornings when he would pick us up, sitting on the curve on Beverly Glen as his car would turn the corner from Sunset Boulevard and we would get in and ride to his ranch and play games and he would always make sure it ended up a tie.

—Michael Reagan, eulogy for his father, June 11, 2004

We don't know what turns our life will take or what doors will open and there is nothing worse than to have such a door open and then learn you gave away your admittance ticket back in your school days.

—Letter to his son Ron at boarding school, 1972, quoted in
REAGAN: A LIFE IN LETTERS edited by Kiron K. Skinner,
Annelise Anderson, and Martin Anderson

My father taught all of his children to ride a bicycle, and he taught us the same way. After the training wheels came off, he would run behind us, holding on to the back of the seat so we would feel secure. One day, without our realizing it, he would let go. I remember looking back, expecting to see him with his hands on the bike, and seeing only the distance I had traveled without him—a ribbon of road behind me, my father standing where he had left me, waving and smiling.

—Patti Davis, *THE LONG GOODBYE* by Patti Davis

When you reach a certain level of celebrity, in whatever field, people begin to think of you as public property. Private as he was in many respects, my father seemed, from his children's jealous perspective, to be alarmingly accepting of that. In fact, he sometimes seemed more comfortable in front of a crowd of total strangers than he did sitting at the dinner table surrounded by family. And why not? While an anonymous audience could usually be counted on for nothing but rapt attention and enthusiastic applause, family frequently made for a tougher room altogether.

—Ron Reagan, *MY FATHER AT 100* by Ron Reagan

Like all parents, we had occasional problems with the
children. All four children had minds of their own, and
in different ways they were all capable of expressing their
independence. Ron and Maureen showed that when they
demanded I act more decisively about the Iran–Contra
situation. I'd always encouraged the children to speak their
minds. I suspect it's never easy for children who grow up
in a family with celebrities, and I'm sure that the added
prominence that fell on the shoulders of the children after
I was elected president didn't make their lives any easier.

—*An American Life: The Autobiography* by Ronald Reagan

Lifeguarding provides one of the best vantage points in the
world to learn about people. During my career at the park,
I saved seventy-seven people. I guarantee you they needed
saving—no lifeguard gets wet without good reason. In my
case it really took an emergency because my job was seven
days a week, and from morning until they got tired
of swimming at night.

—*Where's the Rest of Me?* by Ronald Reagan with Richard G. Hubler

From across the backyard of our house in Sacramento, I can see Dad waving jauntily to the guests at my parents' annual Fourth of July party as he heads inside to change out of the wet clothes plastered to his frame. Has he unaccountably decided to take a swim fully dressed?

With a hurried whisper, my mother fills me in as she follows behind. "Daddy just saved a little girl from drowning!"

Typical.

Not that I remembered, at age nine, ever having seen my father actually rescue anyone before. But I knew about his 77 saves at Lowell Park. Seventy-seven people pulled from the Rock River over the course of seven summers. . . . So there was nothing especially surprising about Dad's jumping into the calm, shallow water of our swimming pool to prevent a child from drowning.

—Ron Reagan, *MY FATHER AT 100* by Ron Reagan

I loved playing on the line: For me, it was probably a marriage made in heaven. It's as fundamental as anything in life—a collision between two bodies, one determined to advance, the other determined to resist; one man against another man, blocking, tackling, breaking through the line.

—*AN AMERICAN LIFE: THE AUTOBIOGRAPHY* by Ronald Reagan

To my mind, nothing compares with the kinship between man and animal you find on the back of a horse. I'm not sure what it is, but there you are, in charge of an animal with more muscle in its neck than you have in your whole body. From the minute the horse takes its first step, every muscle in your own body begins to respond to it; how much of the experience is physical and how much is mental, I don't know, but there's no better place for me to think than on top of a horse.

—*An American Life: The Autobiography* by **Ronald Reagan**

He loved the physical work of the ranch. It was strenuous, but he was a big man—strong, in shape and very muscular—and it energized him to get out of the White House and do that heavy labor and to be in the fresh California air. It's impossible to count the number of hours he spent clearing brush, cutting down trees and in other work at the ranch. In fact, it exasperated the news-hungry White House press corps. After eight years of hearing from the White House press office that Reagan was spending another trip clearing brush and chopping wood, they began to ask just how many trees were actually *up* there.

—**Jim Kuhn**, *Ronald Reagan in Private: A Memoir of My Years in the White House* by **Jim Kuhn**

I usually took a pile of homework and made my weekly radio broadcast during our weekends at Camp David. But there was almost always time to relax in front of a fire with a book. When the weather was right, we'd go swimming; during the summer, we often ate our meals on the patio. There were always a dozen or so members of the White House staff with us, and on Friday and Saturday nights we usually all got together to watch a movie with big baskets of popcorn in front of us.

—*AN AMERICAN LIFE: THE AUTOBIOGRAPHY* by **Ronald Reagan**

EDUCATION, KNOWLEDGE, AND INFORMATION

Education is like a diamond with many facets: It includes the basic mastery of numbers and letters that give us access to the treasury of human knowledge, accumulated and refined through the ages. It includes technical and vocational training, as well as instruction in science, higher mathematics, and humane letters. But no true education can leave out the moral and spiritual dimensions of human life and human striving. Only education that addresses this dimension can lead to that blend of compassion, humility, and understanding that is summed up in one word: *wisdom.*

—Proclamation for Education Day U.S.A., April 19, 1986

Education is not the means of showing people how to get what they want. Education is an exercise by means of which enough men, it is hoped, will learn to want what is worth having.

—Remark quoted in SINCERELY, RONALD REAGAN edited by Helene von Damm

Our leaders must remember that education doesn't begin with some isolated bureaucrat in Washington. It doesn't even begin with state or local officials. Education begins in the home, where it is a parental right and responsibility.

—Address to the National Catholic Educational Association, Chicago, Illinois, April 15, 1982

Loyalty, faithfulness, commitment, courage, patriotism,
the ability to distinguish between right and wrong—
I hope that these values are as much a part of your life as
any calculus course or social science study.

—Remarks at the presentation ceremony for the Presidential Scholars
Awards, the White House, June 16, 1988

As the years pass, if you have let yourselves absorb the spirit
and tradition of this place, you'll find the four years you've
spent here living in your memory as a rich and important
part of your life. Oh, you'll have some regrets along with
the happy memories. I let football and other extracurricular
activities eat into my study time with the result that my
grade average was closer to the C level required for eligibility
than it was to straight A's. And even now I wonder what
I might have accomplished if I'd studied harder.

—Commencement address at Eureka College, Eureka, Illinois,
May 9, 1982

Teachers should be paid and promoted on the basis of
their merit and competence. Hard-earned tax dollars
should encourage the best. They have no business [being]
rewarded for incompetence and mediocrity.

—Address at Seton Hall University, South Orange, New Jersey,
May 21, 1983

Yours is a sacred mission. In the words of Henry Adams, "A teacher affects eternity." Each of you, as tiring and routine as your daily duties may sometimes seem, is a keeper of the American dream, the American future. By informing and exercising young minds, by transmitting learning and values, you are the vital link between all that is most precious in our national heritage and our children and grandchildren, who will some day take up the burdens of guiding the greatest, freest society on Earth.

—Remarks at the annual convention of the American Federation of Teachers, Los Angeles, California, July 5, 1983

Let us go forward with our conviction that education doesn't begin with Washington officials or state officials or local officials. It begins with the family, where it is the right and the responsibility of every parent. And that responsibility, I think, includes teaching children respect for skin color that is different from their own; religious beliefs that are different from their own. It includes conveying the message to the young as well as to the old that racial discrimination and religious bigotry have no place in a free society.

—Remarks at the annual convention of National Religious Broadcasters, Washington, D.C., February 9, 1982

Information is the oxygen of the modern age. It seeps through the walls topped by barbed wire, it wafts across the electrified borders. . . . The Goliath of totalitarianism will be brought down by the David of the microchip.

—Remark quoted in *The Guardian*, June 14, 1989

"To see the universe in a grain of sand" is no longer a poetic metaphor, but the daily reality of the silicon chip. F. Scott Fitzgerald wrote that when the early explorers first looked on this land, they must have held their breath. They had, for the first time in history, come face-to-face with something commensurate with man's infinite capacity for wonder. Yet it was not the last time. We, too, stand on the shores of something as vast—of an economic and technological future immense with promise.

—Remarks at the annual meeting of the Atlantic Council, Washington, D.C., June 13, 1988

American can Remain
e Unless Our
International
HOTEL · LOS ANGELES ·
Freedom Under God
AMERICANISM EDUCATIONAL LEAGUE

RELIGION

God's miracles are to be found in nature itself; the wind and waves, the wood that becomes a tree—all of these are explained biologically, but behind them is the hand of God. And I believe that is true of creation itself.

—Remark quoted in SINCERELY, RONALD REAGAN edited by Helene von Damm

Each of us, each of you, is made in the most enduring, powerful image of Western civilization. We're made in the image of God, the image of God the Creator.

—Remarks to citizens in Hambach, Federal Republic of Germany, May 6, 1985

I have long believed there was a divine plan that placed this land here to be found by people of a special kind, that we have a rendezvous with destiny. Yes, there is a spirit moving in this land and a hunger in the people for a spiritual revival. If the task I seek should be given to me, I would pray only that I could perform it in a way that would serve God.

—Letter written while campaigning for the Republican presidential nomination in 1976, quoted in SINCERELY, RONALD REAGAN edited by Helene von Damm

If we ever forget that we're one nation under God, then we will be a nation gone under.

—Remarks at an ecumenical prayer breakfast, Dallas, Texas, August 23, 1984

The Constitution was never meant to prevent people from praying; its declared purpose was to protect their freedom to pray.

—Address to the nation, September 18, 1982

Prayer, of course, is deeply personal: The way in which it finds expression depends on our individual dispositions as well as on our religious convictions. Just as our religious institutions are guaranteed freedom in this land, so also do we cherish the diversity of our faiths and the freedom afforded to each of us to pray according to the promptings of our individual conscience.

—Proclamation for National Day of Prayer, May 1, 1986

Let us remember that whether we be Christian or Jew
or Moslem, we are all children of Abraham,
we are all children of the same God.

—Remarks upon the visit of Israeli Prime Minister Menachem Begin,
the White House, September 9, 1981

Now, no one is suggesting that others should be forced
into any religious activity, but to prevent those who believe
in God from expressing their faith is an outrage. And
the relentless drive to eliminate God from our schools
can and should be stopped.

—Remarks at a candle-lighting ceremony for prayer in public schools,
September 25, 1982

Dad was also a deeply, unabashedly religious man. But he
never made the fatal mistake of so many politicians wearing
his faith on his sleeve to gain political advantage. True, after
he was shot and nearly killed early in his presidency, he came
to believe that God had spared him in order that he might
do good. But he accepted that as a responsibility, not a
mandate. And there is a profound difference.

—Ron Reagan, eulogy for his father, Ronald Reagan Presidential
Library, Simi Valley, California, June 11, 2004

Getting shot hurts. Still my fear was growing because no matter how hard I tried to breathe it seemed I was getting less & less air. I focused on that tiled ceiling and prayed. But I realized I couldn't ask for God's help while at the same time I felt hatred for the mixed up young man who had shot me. Isn't that the meaning of the lost sheep? We are all God's children & therefore equally beloved by him. I began to pray for his soul and that he would find his way back to the fold. . . . Whatever happens now I owe my life to God and will try to serve him in every way I can.

—Excerpt from Reagan's diary, March 30, 1981, *THE REAGAN DIARIES*, edited by Douglas Brinkley

POVERTY AND RICHES

We always rented our home and never had enough money
for luxuries. But I don't remember suffering because of that.
Although my mother sometimes took in sewing
to supplement my dad's wages and I grew up wearing
my brother's clothes and shoes after he'd outgrown them,
we always had enough to eat and Nelle was forever finding
people who were worse off than we were and going out
of her way to help them.

—*An American Life: The Autobiography* by Ronald Reagan

❧

We were poor when I was young, but the difference then
was the government didn't come around telling you
you were poor.

—Remark quoted in *Time*, July 7, 1986

❧

Maybe it's about time we had a president who remembers the
Great Depression and what it was all about.

—Speech in Birmingham, Michigan, October 16, 1980

❧

Free enterprise has done more to reduce poverty than all the
government programs dreamed up by the Democrats.

—Speech as governor of California, 1972

No one who lived through the Great Depression can ever look upon an unemployed person with anything but compassion. To me, there is no greater tragedy than a breadwinner willing to work, with a job skill but unable to find a market for that job skill. Back in those dark depression days I saw my father on a Christmas Eve open what he thought was a Christmas greeting from his boss. Instead, it was the blue slip telling him he no longer had a job. The memory of him sitting there holding that slip of paper and then saying in a half whisper, "That's quite a Christmas present," it will stay with me as long as I live.

—Speech known as "To Restore America," March 31, 1976

As you look back on that myriad of new federal programs, it's hard to find any that did much good for the poor or the nation as a whole. . . . The waste in dollars and cents was small compared with the waste of human potential. It was squandered by the narcotic of giveaway programs that sapped the human spirit, diminished the incentive of people to work, destroyed families, and produced an increase in female and child poverty, deteriorating schools, and disintegrating neighborhoods. The liberals had had their turn at bat in the 1960s and they had struck out.

—*An American Life: The Autobiography* by Ronald Reagan

Welfare's purpose should be to eliminate, as far as possible, the need for its own existence.

—Interview with the *Los Angeles Times*, January 7, 1970

∾

My friends, some years ago the federal government declared war on poverty—and poverty won.

—State of the Union address, January 25, 1988

∾

The size of the federal budget is not an appropriate barometer of social conscience or charitable concern.

—Remarks at the annual meeting of the National Alliance of Business, October 5, 1981

∾

We're the party that wants to see an America in which people can still get rich.

—Remark at a Republican congressional dinner, May 4, 1982

As I have often said, governments don't produce economic growth, people do. What government *can* do is encourage Americans to tap their well of ingenuity and unleash their entrepreneurial spirit, then get out of the way.

—*AN AMERICAN LIFE: THE AUTOBIOGRAPHY* by Ronald Reagan

WIT AND WISDOM

Reporter: What kind of governor will you be?
Reagan: I don't know; I've never played a governor.

—Remark on being elected governor of California, November 1967

◎

In the business that I used to be in, you learn not to stay on stage too long. You learn there's a time you have to exit.

—Remarked on September 24, 1978

◎

Let it show on the record that when the American people cried out for economic help, Jimmy Carter took refuge behind a dictionary. Well, if it's a definition he wants, I'll give him one. A recession is when your neighbor loses his job. A depression is when you lose yours. And recovery is when Jimmy Carter loses his.

—In response to Carter's gibe that Reagan misused the word *depression*, campaign speech in Jersey City, New Jersey, September 1, 1980

I had a dream the other night. I dreamed that Jimmy Carter
came to me and asked why I wanted his job. I told him
I didn't want his job. I want to be president.

—Remarked in Detroit, Michigan, July 14, 1980

❧

I hope you're all Republicans.

—Remark to surgeons who were about to operate on him after the
assassination attempt, Washington, D.C., March 30, 1981

❧

You can tell a lot about a fellow's character by his way of
eating jelly beans.

—Remark quoted in *The Observer*, March 29, 1981

❧

Tip O'Neill once asked me how I keep myself looking
so young for the cameras. I told him I have a good makeup
team—the same people who've been repairing the
Statue of Liberty.

—Remarked on May 15, 1986

But there are advantages to being elected president.
The day after I was elected, I had my high school grades
classified top secret.

—Remarks at a high school commencement address, Glassboro,
New Jersey, June 19, 1986

How do you tell a Communist? Well, it's someone who reads
Marx and Lenin. And how do you tell an anti-Communist?
It's someone who understands Marx and Lenin.

—Speech in Arlington, Virginia, September 25, 1987

My fellow Americans, I'm pleased to tell you today that
I've signed legislation that will outlaw Russia forever.
We begin bombing in five minutes.

—Remarked, jokingly, into an open microphone that he was unaware
was on, just before a speech that was to be broadcast, August 1984

My fellow Americans, I'm pleased to tell you today that
I've signed legislation that will outlaw Russia forever.
We begin bombing in five minutes.

Before I took up my current line of work, I got to know
a thing or two about negotiating when I represented the
Screen Actors Guild in contract talks with the studios.
After the studios, Gorbachev was a snap.

—Remarks to the National Chamber Foundation, Washington, D.C.,
November 17, 1988

I've laid down the law, though, to everyone from now on about anything that happens: no matter what time it is, wake me, even if it's in the middle of a Cabinet meeting.

—Speech to the White House Correspondents' Association, 1984

∾

You know, in the Soviet Union, for a private citizen to buy an automobile, there is a ten-year waiting period. . . . You have to put the money down too, ten years in advance. So this man has gone in and he's doing all the signing, all the papers and putting out his money. And finally when he makes the final signature the man behind the counter says, "Now, come back in ten years and take delivery." And the man asks, "Morning or afternoon?" And the man behind the counter says, "Well, ten years from now, what difference does it make?" "Well," the man answers, "the plumber's coming in the morning."

—Remarked at a World Affairs Council Meeting, 1988

∾

I want you to know that also I will not make age an issue of this campaign. I am not going to exploit, for political purposes, my opponent's youth and inexperience.

—Remarked during a televised presidential debate between Ronald Reagan and Walter Mondale, Kansas City, Missouri, October 8, 1984

On the whole, I've enjoyed my life as it is. Even when there were setbacks, I recalled my mother saying— "everything happens for a reason and for the best. If you accept what seems a disappointment at the time, there will come a day when you'll look back and see that if it hadn't happened, some of the good things that followed wouldn't have happened."

—Letter replying to correspondent Trude B. Feldman's questions to Reagan upon Reagan's 75th birthday, quoted in *DEAR AMERICANS: LETTERS FROM THE DESK OF RONALD REAGAN* edited by Ralph E. Weber and Ralph A. Weber

I grew up observing how the love and common sense of purpose that unites families is one of the most powerful glues on earth and that it can help them overcome the greatest of adversities. I learned that hard work is an essential part of life—that by and large, you don't get something for nothing—and that America was a place that offered unlimited opportunity to those who did work hard. I learned to admire risk takers and entrepreneurs, be they farmers or small merchants, who went to work and took risks to build something for themselves and their children, pushing at the boundaries of their lives to make them better.

—*AN AMERICAN LIFE: THE AUTOBIOGRAPHY* by Ronald Reagan

My father was orphaned at age six, and I grew up never having heard anything or knowing anything about my family tree, and I would meet other people of the name Reagan or Regan—we're all of the same clan, all cousins. . . . Then I received a letter or a paper from Ireland that told me that in the clan to which we belong, those who said Regan and spelled it that way were the professional people and the educators, and only the common laborers called it Reagan. So, meet a common laborer. . . . My father also, at the same time, used to tell me and my brother when we were boys— very proudly he would say that in this country the Irish built the jails and then filled them. And I was kind of disturbed at the note of pride in his voice because I'd pictured this in a little different way until I finally learned what he was implying: that the great percentage of the police officers in our land are Irish.

—Speech from a luncheon with Ireland's ambassador Sean Donlon, Washington, D.C., March 17, 1981

The future doesn't belong to the fainthearted; it belongs to the brave. The *Challenger* crew was pulling us into the future, and we'll continue to follow them.

—Speech after the loss of the space shuttle *CHALLENGER* and all of its crew, the White House, January 28, 1986

What should happen when you make a mistake is this:
you take your knocks, you learn your lessons,
and then you move on.

—Address to the nation on the Iran–Contra scandal, March 4, 1987

∼

On my desk in the Oval Office, I have a little sign that says:
There is no limit to what a man can do or where he can go
if he doesn't mind who gets the credit.

—Remarks at a meeting of the White House Conference for a
Drug Free America, February 29, 1988

∼

Because we are a great nation, our challenges seem complex.
It will always be this way. But as long as we remember
our first principles and believe in ourselves, the future
will always be ours.

—Farewell address to the nation, January 11, 1989

The history of our civilization, the great advances that made it possible, is not a story of cynics or doom criers. It is a gallant chronicle of the optimists, the determined people, men and women who dreamed great dreams and dared to try whatever it took to make them come true.

—Remarks at the dedication of the California State Water Project's Perris Dam, Riverside, California, May 18, 1973

I, too, have been described as an undying optimist, always seeing a glass half full when some see it as half empty. And, yes, it's true—I always see the sunny side of life. And that's not just because I've been blessed by achieving so many of my dreams. My optimism comes not just from my strong faith in God, but from my strong and enduring faith in man.

—Remarks at the dedication of the Ronald Reagan Presidential Library, Simi Valley, California, November 4, 1991

To grasp and hold a vision, that is the very essence of successful leadership—not only on the movie set where I learned it, but everywhere.

—Remark quoted in *The Wilson Quarterly*, Winter 1994

The explorers of the modern era are the entrepreneurs, men with vision, with the courage to take risks and faith enough to brave the unknown. These entrepreneurs and their small enterprises are responsible for almost all the economic growth in the United States. They are the prime movers of the technological revolution. In fact, one of the largest personal computer firms in the United States was started by two college students, no older than you, in the garage behind their home. Some people, even in my own country, look at the riot of experiment that is the free market and see only waste. What of all the entrepreneurs that fail? Well, many do, particularly the successful ones; often several times. And if you ask them the secret of their success, they'll tell you it's all that they learned in their struggles along the way; yes, it's what they learned from failing. Like an athlete in competition or a scholar in pursuit of the truth, experience is the greatest teacher. And that's why it's so hard for government planners, no matter how sophisticated, to ever substitute for millions of individuals working night and day to make their dreams come true.

—Address at Moscow State University, May 31, 1988

∾

Life is one grand, sweet song, so start the music.

—Attributed

A leader, once convinced a particular course of action is the right one, must have the determination to stick with it and be undaunted when the going gets rough.

—Address to the Cambridge Union Society, Cambridge, England, December 5, 1990

❧

Whatever else history may say about me when I'm gone, I hope it will record that I appealed to your best hopes, not your worst fears; to your confidence rather than your doubts. My dream is that you will travel the road ahead with liberty's lamp guiding your steps and opportunity's arm steadying your way.

—Remarks at the Republican National Convention, Houston, Texas, August 17, 1992

❧

My philosophy of life is that if we make up our mind what we are going to make of our lives, then work hard toward that goal, we never lose—somehow we win out.

—Attributed

From time to time I have been called the Great
Communicator. But I'll tell you, it's no easy thing
to communicate what I feel right now.

—Remarks upon receiving the Presidential Medal of Freedom,
Washington, D.C., January 13, 1993

∾

There's a tendency to throw aside old values as belonging to
an earlier generation. Don't discard those values that have
proven, over the period of time, their value. Just believe in
those values that made our nation great and keep them:
faith, family, hard work, and, above all, freedom.

—Speech at the Illinois State Fair, Springfield, Illinois, August 12, 1986

∾

I never thought of myself as a great man, just a man
committed to great ideas. I've always believed that
individuals should take priority over the state. History
has taught me that this is what sets America apart—not
to remake the world in our image, but to inspire people
everywhere with a sense of their own boundless possibilities.
There's no question I am an idealist, which is another
way of saying I am an American.

—Letter to Peggy Noonan in response to her questions about
his view of his leadership, quoted in *WHEN CHARACTER WAS KING:
A STORY OF RONALD REAGAN* by Peggy Noonan

Letter to the American People
November 5, 1994

My Fellow Americans,

I have recently been told that I am one of the millions of Americans who will be afflicted with Alzheimer's Disease.

Upon learning this news, Nancy & I had to decide whether as private citizens we would keep this a private matter or whether we would make this news known in a public way.

In the past Nancy suffered from breast cancer and I had my cancer surgeries. We found through our open disclosures we were able to raise public awareness. We were happy that as a result many more people underwent testing. They were treated in early stages and able to return to normal, healthy lives.

So now, we feel it is important to share it with you. In opening our hearts, we hope this might promote greater awareness of this condition. Perhaps it will encourage a clearer understanding of the individuals and families who are affected by it.

At the moment I feel just fine. I intend to live the remainder of the years God gives me on this earth doing the things I have always done. I will continue to share life's journey with my beloved Nancy and my family. I plan to enjoy the great outdoors and stay in touch with my friends and supporters.

Unfortunately, as Alzheimer's Disease progresses, the family often bears a heavy burden. I only wish there was some way I could spare Nancy from this painful experience. When the time comes I am confident that with your help she will face it with faith and courage.

In closing let me thank you, the American people for giving me the great honor of allowing me to serve as your President. When the Lord calls me home, whenever that may be, I will leave with the greatest love for this country of ours and eternal optimism for its future.

I now begin this journey that will lead me into the sunset of my life. I know that for America there will always be a bright dawn ahead.

Thank you my friends. May God always bless you.

Sincerely,
Ronald Reagan

THE LEGACY OF
RONALD REAGAN

My father was fearless—he took a bullet and made a joke as he walked into the hospital; he recovered from that near-fatal wound with no bitterness toward the man who tried to kill him. Suddenly, in the eighties, we considered fearlessness an option. We believed Jimmy Carter's bleak perspective; in 1984, we believed Mondale's warnings. But we wanted to believe in Ronald Reagan's shimmering vision of a better place.

—Patti Davis, *The Long Goodbye* by Patti Davis

My husband loved being president. He *enjoyed* it, all of it—the decision-making, the responsibilities, the negotiating, as well as the ceremonies, the public appearances, and the meetings. As George Will has said, Ronald Reagan has a talent for happiness.

—Nancy Reagan, *My Turn: The Memoirs of Nancy Reagan* by Nancy Reagan with William Novak

A paradoxical character, my father: He was warm yet remote. As affable as they come, he had, in his later life, virtually no close friends besides his wife. He thrived on public display, yet remained intensely private. Forceful in the role of political leader, he was, in person, surprisingly soft-spoken and gentle.

—Ron Reagan, *My Father at 100* by Ron Reagan

We have all noticed in life that big people with big virtues not infrequently have big flaws, too. Reagan's great flaw it seemed to me, and seems to me, was not one of character but personality. That was his famous detachment, which was painful for his children and disorienting for his staff. No one around him quite understood it, the deep and emotional engagement in public events and public affairs, and the slight and seemingly formal interest in the lives of those around him. James Baker III called him the kindest and most impersonal man he'd ever known, and there was some truth to that. . . .

—Peggy Noonan, *CHARACTER ABOVE ALL, VOLUME 6* by Peggy Noonan, edited by Robert A. Wilson

In Washington, socializing is regarded as part of the job, an extension of the business day, but that went against Ronnie's grain. He believed that parties and dinners are for fun, not work, and in most social situations he prefers to tell stories. That would always put a gathering on a more informal plane, where political talk—or gossip, which Ronnie hates—seemed like an intrusion.

—Nancy Reagan, *MY TURN: THE MEMOIRS OF NANCY REAGAN* by Nancy Reagan with William Novak

Part of his success, of course, was his electability—his immense personal appeal and his ability to communicate his vision to millions of Americans. Although he didn't talk much about it publicly, he believed his Hollywood background played a big role in that success. Late in his second term, I heard him say that if it hadn't been for his Hollywood experience, "I don't know how I'd be able to do this job." . . . He was also gifted at governing and, among politicians, those skills often don't come in tandem. Reagan had both—electability and governing skills.

His adroitness at governing grew out of his unparalleled ability to stay focused on his ultimate goals and avoid getting sidetracked from his agenda. His was leadership at its best.

—Jim Kuhn, *RONALD REAGAN IN PRIVATE: A MEMOIR OF MY YEARS IN THE WHITE HOUSE* by Jim Kuhn

But Ronnie's easygoing manner is deceiving. Although he isn't as driven or as intense as some of his predecessors in the White House, underneath the calm exterior is a tenacious, stubborn, and very competitive man. Just look at the record: Ronnie rarely loses.

—Nancy Reagan, *MY TURN: THE MEMOIRS OF NANCY REAGAN* by Nancy Reagan with William Novak

Reagan is always described as genial and easygoing, but Marty Anderson used to call him "warmly ruthless." He would do in the nicest possible way what had to be done. He was as nice as he could be about it, but he knew where he was going, and if you were in the way you were gone. And you might argue his ruthlessness made everything possible.

—Peggy Noonan, *Character Above All, Volume 6* by Peggy Noonan, edited by Robert A. Wilson

Reagan would hear the criticisms, putdowns and insults and shrug, and sometimes laugh. Sometimes he'd grimace slightly and shake his head. I always thought criticism hurt him now and then, but never made an impression on him. He wasn't up nights thrashing around being angry. It didn't get to his core the way it got to Nixon's and LBJ's. Criticism didn't inspire him to take action to deflect or mollify or defy. He became expert at the shrug and the laugh. . . .

—Peggy Noonan, *When Character Was King: A Story of Ronald Reagan* by Peggy Noonan

He always appreciated the simple truth of human feelings, of relationships. As entrenched as he was in politics, he relished the moments when ideology was set aside and a bridge was formed between people. He delighted in recounting how he and Gorbachev liked each other as men and related to each other as two people who had come from humble beginnings to stand face-to-face in the spotlight of history at a crucial time. They forged a friendship; to my father, that said everything.

—Patti Davis, *THE LONG GOODBYE* by Patti Davis

He was firmly a conservative—and had been for 40 years—but he was pragmatic. He had no hesitation in hiring former adversaries or going against his most passionate supporters if he could achieve his ultimate goals and fulfill the promises he had made to the American people. For his staff and cabinet choices, he chose the best people for the job, even though some of those choices didn't win kudos from his most committed supporters.

—Jim Kuhn, *RONALD REAGAN IN PRIVATE: A MEMOIR OF MY YEARS IN THE WHITE HOUSE* by Jim Kuhn

His admirable quality was if he gave you his word you could sleep very well that night.

—Dan Rostenkowski, former chairman of the House Ways and Means Committee, quoted in *WHEN CHARACTER WAS KING* by Peggy Noonan

❧

Even his gaffes tended to contribute to the sense that this man was real.

—Richard Norton Smith, interview on *NEWSHOUR WITH JIM LEHRER* about Reagan's legacy, June 7, 2004

❧

We often disagreed on issues of the day, but I had immense respect and admiration for his leadership and his extraordinary ability to inspire the nation to live up to its high ideals. The warmth of his personality always shone through, and his infectious optimism gave us all the feeling that it really was "morning in America." On foreign policy he will be honored as the President who won the Cold War, and his "Mr. Gorbachev, tear down this wall" will be linked forever with President Kennedy's "Ich bin ein Berliner."

—Ted Kennedy

I never heard anyone say that Ronald Reagan was anything but polite. He spoke to everyone with the same gentleness— waiters, presidents, security guards—whomever. He was always a gentleman—no wonder George loved him!

—Barbara Bush, *Recollections of Reagan: A Portrait of Ronald Reagan* edited by Peter Hannaford

He was always busy with something important. I never saw him when he wasn't working—reading, writing, dealing with significant issues or policy matters—whether it was in the White House residence or Oval Office, on Air Force One or Marine One, at Camp David, in hotel suites in the United States and around the world. He was a voracious reader, and he also loved to write. At the end of the workday at the White House, he always went upstairs with a stack of briefing material to get through that evening, and he always came down the next day having read everything and knowing it all. Every time I saw President Reagan over the four years of his second term, he was working. He never just relaxed or watched television, and I never saw him take a nap. At Camp David, the television was usually on just for Sunday-morning talk shows or various other news shows.

—Jim Kuhn, *Ronald Reagan in Private: A Memoir of My Years in the White House* by Jim Kuhn

As prime minister, I worked closely with Ronald Reagan for
eight of the most important years of all of our lives.
We talked regularly both before and after his presidency.
And I have had time and cause to reflect on what made him a
great president. Ronald Reagan knew his own mind. He had
firm principles—and, I believe, right ones. He expounded
them clearly, he acted upon them decisively. When the
world threw problems at the White House, he was not
baffled, or disorientated, or overwhelmed. He knew almost
instinctively what to do. . . . Nothing was more typical of
Ronald Reagan than that large-hearted magnanimity—and
nothing was more American. Therein lies perhaps the final
explanation of his achievements. Ronald Reagan carried
the American people with him in his great endeavors
because there was perfect sympathy between them.
He and they loved America and what it stands for—
freedom and opportunity for ordinary people.

—Margaret Thatcher, eulogy for President Reagan, Washington, D.C.,
June 11, 2004

He presented some very concise, very clear messages that
appealed to the American people. I think throughout his
term in office he was very worthy of the moniker that was
put on him as the "Great Communicator."

—Jimmy Carter

Even when he was breaking Democrats' hearts, he did so with a smile and in the spirit of honest and open debate. The differences were real, but because of the way President Reagan led, he taught us that there is a big difference between strong beliefs and bitter partisanship.

—John Kerry

❧

Hillary and I will always remember President Ronald Reagan for the way he personified the indomitable optimism of the American people, and for keeping America at the forefront of the fight for freedom for people everywhere. It is fitting that a piece of the Berlin Wall adorns the Ronald Reagan Building in Washington.

—Bill Clinton

❧

Pride in our country, respect for our armed services, a healthy appreciation for the dangers beyond our borders, an insistence that there was no easy equivalence between East and West—in all this I had no quarrel with Reagan. And when the Berlin Wall came tumbling down, I had to give the old man his due, even if I never gave him my vote.

—Barack Obama, *THE AUDACITY OF HOPE: THOUGHTS ON RECLAIMING THE AMERICAN DREAM* by Barack Obama

As his vice president for eight years, I learned more from
Ronald Reagan than from anyone I encountered in all my
years of public life. I learned kindness; we all did. I also
learned courage; the nation did. . . . And he fought hard for
his beliefs. But he led from conviction, but never made an
adversary into an enemy. He was never mean-spirited. . . .
God bless you, Ronald Wilson Reagan, and the nation
you loved and led so well.

—George Bush, eulogy for President Reagan, Washington, D.C.,
June 11, 2004

He came to office with great hopes for America, and more
than hopes—like the president he had revered and once
saw in person, Franklin Roosevelt, Ronald Reagan matched
an optimistic temperament with bold, persistent action.
President Reagan was optimistic about the great promise
of economic reform, and he acted to restore the reward and
spirit of enterprise. He was optimistic that a strong America
could advance the peace, and he acted to build the strength
that mission required. He was optimistic that liberty would
thrive wherever it was planted, and he acted to defend
liberty wherever it was threatened.

—George W. Bush, eulogy for President Reagan, Washington, D.C.,
June 11, 2004

I recall with deep gratitude the late president's unwavering commitment to the service of the nation and to the cause of freedom as well as his abiding faith in the human and spiritual values which ensure a future of solidarity, justice, and peace in our world.

—**Pope John Paul II**

I don't know whether we would have been able to agree and to insist on the implementation of our agreements with a different person at the helm of American government. True, Reagan was a man of the right. But, while adhering to his convictions, with which one could agree or disagree, he was not dogmatic; he was looking for negotiations and cooperation. And this was the most important thing to me: he had the trust of the American people.

—**Mikhail Gorbachev, "A President Who Listened,"**
THE NEW YORK TIMES, **June 7, 2004**

A great statesman who through the strength of his convictions and his commitment to democracy will leave a deep mark on history.

—**French President Jacques Chirac**

I take the death of Ronald Reagan very hard. He was a man whom fate set by me in perhaps the most difficult years at the end of the twentieth century. He has already entered history as a man who was instrumental in bringing about the end of the Cold War. . . . It was his goal and his dream to end his term and enter history as a peacemaker.

—Soviet Prime Minister Mikhail Gorbachev

His engagement in overcoming the East–West conflict and his vision of a free and united Europe created the conditions for change that in the end made the restoration of German unity possible.

—German Chancellor Gerhard Schröder

President Reagan was the Churchill of his era. His commitment to the principles of freedom and democracy and his boundless optimism for humanity will remain an inspiration for us all.

—Canadian Prime Minister Stephen Harper

Big as he was, he never tried to make anyone feel small.
Powerful as he became, he never took advantage of those
who were weaker. Strength, he believed, was never more
admirable than when it was applied with restraint.
Shopkeeper, doorman, king or queen, it made no difference,
Dad treated everyone with the same unfailing courtesy.
Acknowledging the innate dignity in us all.

—Ron Reagan, eulogy for his father, Ronald Reagan Presidential
Library, Simi Valley, California, June 11, 2004

I've never met anybody like my father, and I don't think
this country will see another man like him anytime soon.
He's the warmest person I've ever come across, and it's a
warmth that runs so deep inside him it just kind of pulls
you along like a magnet. People respond to that in him—
perfect strangers, even—and if he can get that kind of
response out of just plain folks on the street, just imagine
what he does for the people who know him.

—Maureen Reagan, *First Father, First Daughter: A Memoir*
by Maureen Reagan

I believe when people think of his courage, they think first of what happened that day in March 1981 when he was shot. He tried to walk into the hospital himself but his knees buckled and he had to be helped. They put him on a gurney, and soon he started the one-liners. Quoting Churchill, he reminded everyone that there's nothing so exhilarating as to be shot at without effect. . . . But Reagan the political figure had a form of courage that I think is the hardest and most demanding kind. A general will tell you that anyone can be brave for five minutes; the adrenaline pumps, you do things of which you wouldn't have thought yourself capable. But Reagan had that harder and more exhausting courage, the courage to swim against the tide. And we all forget it now because he changed the tide. Looking back, we forget that the political mood of today, in which he might find himself quite comfortable, is quite different from the political mood the day he walked into politics.

—Peggy Noonan, *CHARACTER ABOVE ALL, VOLUME 6* by Peggy Noonan, edited by Robert A. Wilson

All in all, I think Ronald Reagan's most important contributions to the nation were his decency, his sense of honor, and the deep feeling he conveyed to the entire world that America is the greatest country on the face of the earth.

—George Bush, *RECOLLECTIONS OF REAGAN: A PORTRAIT OF RONALD REAGAN* edited by Peter Hannaford

I believe that, as we move forward toward the next century, a careful look at the Reagan legacy and President Reagan's leadership can provide the guidelines for a future in which we have peace, freedom, and the flourishing of the human spirit, which will be a benefit not only to the United States but the whole world.

—Edwin Meese III, speech at Ashland University, Ashland, Ohio, 1999

He really probably more than any president since FDR transformed the political landscape, and that's not easy to do. FDR shattered the political consensus that he found in place in 1933, and he left behind a new consensus and an army of followers who for 50 years really defined American politics. And Ronald Reagan really followed in his footsteps, even if they charted a different course.

—Richard Norton Smith, interview on *NEWSHOUR WITH JIM LEHRER* about Reagan's legacy, June 7, 2004

I think he did expand the boundaries of freedom in this country and overseas, he rebuilt the American presidency. . . . I think he [convinced] us that once again that the future of the best, our best days were always ahead of us.

—David Gergen, interview on *NEWSHOUR WITH JIM LEHRER* about Reagan's legacy, June 7, 2004

His constant refrain throughout his time in the White House was that government was becoming too big, too inefficient, too unresponsive and too wasteful. As governor, Reagan demonstrated the ability to exercise fiscal restraint and he urged leaders in Congress to do the same thing.

I think it appropriate that we are celebrating Reagan's 100th birthday at time when national debt and the deficit are at an all-time high. While we know that Reagan possessed the willingness to tackle such issues, I believe the lesson we can learn most from his presidency is the endlessly optimistic attitude he had that the United States and its people would meet challenges of the day and emerge stronger because of the struggle to overcome. His assertion that America was "the shining city on a hill" guided him, as it should us. A hard-nosed, gritty politician, Reagan would have jumped at the chance to take on the responsibility of leading this country out of this recession, just as he did in 1981. So as we celebrate Ronald Reagan's 100th birthday, let us take a moment to reflect upon the life of a man who, as president, always did what was necessary to move the country forward in the way he felt was most beneficial to those who mattered most, the people.

—Illinois Senator Mark Kirk, speech from the Senate floor commemorating Reagan's 100th birthday, February 2011

He had not only changed the country but also the world.
The American economic boom had given birth to a
technological boom that was spreading around the globe,
and more and more countries were moving toward freedom
and democracy. And not, as Reagan would say and as he
truly felt, because of him but because the ideas of the
founders, whose centuries-old ideas had lost none
of their power with the passing of time.

—Peggy Noonan, *When Character Was King: A Story of
Ronald Reagan* by Peggy Noonan

I think he transcended his time. He was both a traditionalist,
someone who for millions of people who felt that our culture
was adrift—embodied what we call traditional values—but
he was also a visionary; he was a man, you had a sense
he couldn't wait to get to the 21st century just to see
all of his belief in the future confirmed.

—Richard Norton Smith, interview on *NewsHour with Jim Lehrer*
about Reagan's legacy, June 7, 2004

I know in my heart that man is good, that what is right will
always eventually triumph, and that there is purpose and
worth to each and every life.

—Reagan's words, inscribed at his burial site

CHRONOLOGY

FEBRUARY 6, 1911—Ronald Wilson Reagan is born in Tampico, Illinois, to parents Nelle Wilson Reagan and John Edward Reagan (Jack). It is a difficult delivery, and Nelle Reagan is advised by her doctor not to have any other children. The Reagans are also parents to son Neil, who was born two years earlier.

1920—After several moves in Illinois, the Reagans settle in Dixon, Illinois.

1926—Reagan takes a summer job as a lifeguard at Lowell Park on the Rock River. During the seven summers he works there, he saves seventy-seven people from drowning.

1928—Reagan graduates from Dixon High School. While there, he is student body president; is active in football, basketball, and track; and also takes part in school plays.

1932—Reagan graduates from Eureka College in Eureka, Illinois, with a degree in economics and sociology. He gets a job as a radio announcer at WOC in Davenport, Iowa, which leads to a broadcasting position at WHO in Des Moines, Iowa, where he re-creates the baseball games of the Chicago Cubs and the Chicago White Sox from the studio and gains exposure in the national media.

1937—Reagan enlists as a private in the Army Reserve but is quickly promoted to second lieutenant in the Officers Reserve Corps of the Cavalry. On a visit to California while working at WHO, Reagan meets with an agent and within days receives an offer from Warner Brothers for a seven-year contract starting at two hundred dollars per week. He makes his first picture, *Love Is on the Air*. Reagan goes on to make more than fifty motion pictures over the next twenty years.

1940—In January, Reagan marries actress Jane Wyman. He also makes his most famous film, *Knute Rockne: All American*, about famed Notre Dame legend George Gipp.

1941—Daughter Maureen is born.

1942—Reagan is called to active duty by the Army Air Forces. Assigned to the First Motion Picture Unit in Culver City, California, he makes more than four hundred training films.

1945—The Reagans adopt their son Michael Edward. Reagan signs a million-dollar contract with Warner Brothers; he is honorably discharged from the army with a rank of captain.

1947—Reagan is elected president of the Screen Actors Guild. He goes on to hold the position a total of seven times. Reagan testifies as a friendly witness before the House Committee on Un-American Activities.

1948—Reagan and Jane Wyman divorce.

1952—Reagan, still a Democrat, campaigns for Dwight D. Eisenhower. He marries actress Nancy Davis. Daughter Patricia Ann is born.

1954—Reagan becomes host of *The General Electric Theater* and a spokesperson for the company. As part of his job, he travels around the country to GE plants and gives speeches. He meets with more than 250,000 GE employees over the course of his eight-year employment.

1958—Son Ronald Prescott is born.

1960—Reagan campaigns as a Democrat for Richard Nixon for president.

1962—Reagan officially becomes a Republican.

OCTOBER 27, 1964—Reagan delivers a televised address in support of Republican presidential candidate Barry Goldwater. The speech, known as "A Time for Choosing," is the unofficial start of Reagan's political career.

1965—Reagan's first autobiography, *Where's the Rest of Me?*, is published. The title is taken from a line in Reagan's 1942 movie *Kings Row*.

1966—Reagan is elected the Republican governor of California, winning a landslide election against incumbent governor Edmund G. "Pat" Brown.

1968—Reagan enters the Republican presidential primary as a favorite-son candidate but later supports the nomination of Richard Nixon.

1970—Reagan is reelected as governor of California.

1974—Reagan leaves office after completing his second term as California governor. He begins a radio talk show and a syndicated column about the issues of concern to him.

1976—Reagan loses by a narrow margin to Gerald Ford for the Republican Party's presidential nomination. Reagan campaigns for Ford and continues with his newspaper column and radio commentary.

1979—Reagan announces his candidacy for president. He wins the Republican nomination and picks George Bush as his running mate.

1980—Reagan wins the election in a landslide against Jimmy Carter. He wins forty-four states in the general election, and the Republicans gain control of the Senate for the first time since 1964.

JANUARY 20, 1981—Reagan is inaugurated as America's 40th president. Iran releases the fifty-two remaining hostages who had been held at the U.S. embassy in Tehran for 444 days.

MARCH 30, 1981—Reagan is shot in an assassination attempt by John Hinckley, Jr., outside of a Washington hotel. Reagan is operated on and makes a full recovery. Three others, including Reagan's press secretary, James Brady, are wounded in the attack.

JULY 29, 1981—Congress passes Reagan's tax bill, which results in 25 percent tax cut over three years.

SEPTEMBER 1981—Reagan appoints Sandra Day O'Connor to the U.S. Supreme Court, the first woman Supreme Court justice.

FALL 1982—The United States experiences the worst recession since the Great Depression. More than nine million Americans are unemployed.

JANUARY 31, 1983—Reagan submits his fiscal 1984 budget to Congress. A $189 billion budget gap is projected resulting from the recession, tax cuts, and increased defense spending. Reagan holds firm on refusing to raise taxes or cut defense spending.

MARCH 23, 1983—Reagan announces his proposal for the Strategic Defense Initiative, later known as "Star Wars," in a nationally televised speech.

OCTOBER 23, 1983—U.S. Marine Corps barracks are bombed in Lebanon, and 241 people are killed. In early 1984, Reagan brings home the remaining marines.

OCTOBER 25, 1983—U.S. troops invade Grenada to oust Marxist rebels and protect several hundred U.S. medical students. After several days of fighting, U.S. forces gain victory.

NOVEMBER 4, 1984—Reagan defeats Walter Mondale in a landslide victory in which he carries forty-nine states, 525 electoral votes, and 59 percent of the popular vote.

JANUARY 20, 1985—Reagan is sworn in for his second term as president. At age 73, he is the oldest president ever to be sworn in.

NOVEMBER 19, 1985—Reagan and Gorbachev meet in Geneva for a summit. Though they disagree on the Strategic Defense

Initiative, they agree to meet again and seek a 50 percent cut in nuclear arms.

JANUARY 28, 1986—The U.S. space shuttle *Challenger* explodes.

MARCH 4, 1987—Reagan addresses the nation about the Iran–Contra affair and acknowledges that mistakes had been made.

JUNE 12, 1987—In a speech at the Brandenburg Gate, Reagan challenges Gorbachev to "tear down this wall."

DECEMBER 1987—Reagan and Gorbachev sign the Intermediate-Range Nuclear Forces Treaty (INF) to eliminate 4 percent of the superpowers' nuclear weapons.

MAY 27, 1988—The Senate ratifies the INF treaty.

NOVEMBER 8, 1988—Vice President George Bush defeats Michael Dukakis to become the 41st U.S. president.

JANUARY 11, 1989—Reagan gives his farewell address to the nation. When he leaves the White House on January 20, he has the highest approval rating of any president since Franklin Delano Roosevelt. He continues to travel, meets with world leaders, gives speeches, and writes his second autobiography.

NOVEMBER 1989—The Berlin Wall comes down, allowing free movement between East and West Germany. A six-thousand-pound section of it is sent to Reagan for his presidential library.

DECEMBER 1991—The Soviet Union is dissolved.

NOVEMBER 5, 1994—Reagan sends an open letter to Americans revealing that he has been diagnosed with Alzheimer's disease and will be retiring from public life.

AUGUST 8, 2001—Reagan's eldest daughter, Maureen, dies after a prolonged battle with cancer.

JUNE 5, 2004—Ronald Reagan dies in California at the age of 93.